Successful Aging in a Rural Community in Japan

CAROLINA ACADEMIC PRESS
Medical Anthropology Series
Pamela J. Stewart *and* Andrew Strathern
Series Editors

Curing and Healing
Medical Anthropology in Global Perspective, Second Edition
Andrew Strathern and Pamela J. Stewart

Physicians at Work, Patients in Pain
Biomedical Practice and Patient Response in Mexico, Second Edition
Kaja Finkler

Endangered Species
Health, Illness, and Death Among Madagascar's People of the Forest
Janice Harper

The Practice of Concern
Ritual, Well-Being, and Aging in Rural Japan
John W. Traphagan

The Gene and the Genie
Tradition, Medicalization and Genetic Counseling
in a Bedouin Community in Israel
Aviad E. Raz

Social Discord and Bodily Disorders
Healing Among the Yupno of Papua New Guinea
Verena Keck

Indigenous Peoples and Diabetes
Community Empowerment and Wellness
edited by Mariana Leal Ferreira and Gretchen Chesley Lang

We Have No Microbes Here
Healing Practices in a Turkish Black Sea Village
Sylvia Wing Önder

Of Orderlies and Men
Hospital Porters Achieving Wellness at Work
Nigel Rapport

Lost Selves and Lonely Persons
Experiences of Illness and Well-Being among Tamil Refugees in Norway
Anne Sigfrid Grønseth

Vulnerability and the Art of Protection
Embodiment and Health Care in Moroccan Households
Marybeth J. MacPhee

Genetic Disorders and Islamic Identity among British Bangladeshis
Santi Rozario

A Tale of an Amulet
Ariela Popper-Giveon

Living Well in Los Duplex
Critical Reflections on Medicalization, Migration and Health Sovereignty
Anna Waldstein

Wellbeing Machine
How Health Emerges from the Assemblages of Everyday Life
Kim McLeod

Tibetan Medicine, Buddhism and Psychiatry
Mental Health and Healing in a Tibetan Exile Community
Susannah Deane

Living in the Tension
Care, Selfhood, and Wellbeing among Faith-Based Youth Workers
Susan Wardell

Adventure as Education
John W. Bennett and Anthropology in the Early Twentieth Century
Laura L. Cochrane

Chronic Illness in a Pakistani Labour Diaspora
Kaveri Qureshi

The Maintenance of Life
Preventing Social Death through Euthanasia Talk and End-of-Life Care—
Lessons from The Netherlands, Second Edition
Frances Norwood

Mobilities of Wellbeing
Migration, the State and Medical Knowledge
edited by Anne Sigfrid Grønseth and Jonathan Skinner

Successful Aging in a Rural Community in Japan
Kimiko Tanaka and Nan E. Johnson

Successful Aging in a Rural Community in Japan

Kimiko Tanaka
ASSOCIATE PROFESSOR OF SOCIOLOGY
DEPARTMENT OF SOCIOLOGY AND ANTHROPOLOGY
JAMES MADISON UNIVERSITY

Nan E. Johnson
PROFESSOR EMERITA
DEPARTMENT OF SOCIOLOGY
MICHIGAN STATE UNIVERSITY

Carolina Academic Press
Durham, North Carolina

Library of Congress Cataloging-in-Publication Data

Names: Tanaka, Kimiko, author. | Johnson, Nan E., author.
Title: Successful aging in a rural community in Japan / by Kimiko Tanaka,
    Nan E. Johnson.
Description: Durham, North Carolina : Carolina Academic Press, [2021] |
    Series: Ethnographic studies in medical anthropology series | Includes
    bibliographical references.
Identifiers: LCCN 2021017720 (print) | LCCN 2021017721 (ebook) | ISBN
    9781531018610 (paperback) | ISBN 9781531018627 (ebook)
Subjects: LCSH: Rural elderly—Japan—Social conditions. | Aging—Social
    aspects—Japan. | Population aging—Japan. | Japan—Rural conditions.
Classification: LCC HQ1064.J3 T384 2021 (print) | LCC HQ1064.J3 (ebook) |
    DDC 305.260952—dc23
LC record available at https://lccn.loc.gov/2021017720
LC ebook record available at https://lccn.loc.gov/2021017721

Carolina Academic Press
700 Kent Street
Durham, North Carolina 27701
(919) 489-7486
www.cap-press.com

Printed in the United States of America

Kimiko Tanaka dedicates her work to her grandparents and parents
who emphasized the importance of women's education,
her spouse who strongly believes in gender equality,
and her daughters who love to read.

Nan E. Johnson dedicates her work on this book in loving memory
of her parents, Joseph Van and Catherine Wood Johnson,
and in honor of her sister, Dr. Kay Johnson McCrary,
who are examples of successful aging.

Contents

Series Editors' Preface

    Lessons in Living: Social Capital in Kawanehonchō , Japan

    Andrew Strathern and Pamela J. Stewart   xiii

Acknowledgments   xvii

Introduction   xix

Chapter 1 · Rural Japan — Facing Demographic Challenges   3

    Causes and Consequences of Dramatic Postwar

        Fertility Decline   5

    Understanding Rural Aging through *"seken"*   10

    Government's Response to Rural Depopulation   11

    Greater Responsibility for Municipal Governments in

        Promoting Healthy Aging   13

    The Importance of Uniqueness in Understanding Rural Aging   16

    Summary   19

Chapter 2 · Kawanehonchō: Structural Support for Rural Aging   21

    Kawanehonchō: An Attractive Rural Town for Elderly People

        to Age in Place   22

    Getting Further Insights on Kawanehonchō Based on

        Recent Censuses   28

    Structural Support for Healthy Aging   30

    Overview of Kawanehonchō Municipal Welfare Office (*Yakuba*)   31

    Overview of the Kawanehonchō Council of Social Welfare (*Shakyō*)   33

Grassroots Programs Supporting the Elderly   35

Summary   35

Chapter 3 · Social Capital, Collective Efficacy, and Elderly Vitality   37

Collective Efficacy and Social Capital   38

The Need for Qualitative Study beyond the West   44

Summary   45

Chapter 4 · Research Methods and Data Collection   47

Surveys Conducted by Municipal Welfare Office and
Kawanehonchō Council of Social Welfare (KCSW)   48

Secondary Data Obtained from Shizuoka Prefecture   48

Observation of the Activities, Facilities, and Programs   48

Interviews with Local Leaders   49

Survey of the Elderly Participating in the Programs   50

Interviews of People Newly Migrated to Surrounding Areas   51

Summary   52

Chapter 5 · Identifying Strengths and Challenges through
Existing Surveys   53

Identifying the Needs through the Survey and Focus Groups
by KCSW   53

Learning from Surveys — Kawanehonchō Municipal Office   55

Frequent Use of Surveys to Improve Organizations   56

Learning from the Survey Conducted by Shizuoka Prefecture   57

Summary   66

Chapter 6 · Connecting the Elderly to the Neighborhood
Community   67

Genki Hatsuratsu Kyōshitsu at Salons   67

Carer's Café   75

Ikigai Day Service Center (IkiDay)   76

Konagai Salon Hustle   79

Quoits Tournament and the Exercise Group (*Genki-Up*)   81

Summary   84

Chapter 7 · Interview with Local Leaders   87

   Otagaisama   87

   Local Festivals   89

   Emphasis on Life Course Perspective in Providing Care for
the Elderly with Dementia   89

   Taking a Walk in Other People's Shoes   91

   Importance of Not Making Assumptions   92

   Concerns for the Future   94

   Summary   95

Chapter 8 · Understanding Characteristics of the Elderly
Participants   97

   Summary   110

Chapter 9 · Elder Migration and the Future of Rural Japan   111

   Rural Inmigration (I-turn) in Japan   112

   Continuing Care Retirement Communities (CCRCs)   117

   The Possibility of a CCRC in Kawanehonchō   119

   Who Are the Newcomers?   120

   Signs of Young People's I-Turn to Kawanehonchō   126

   Summary   128

Chapter 10 · Rural Depopulation and Healthy Aging   129

   Revitalizing Rural Towns   132

   Recommendations for Future Research   136

Endnotes   139

Bibliography   141

Index   165

Series Editors' Preface

Lessons in Living: Social Capital in Kawanehonchō, Japan

Andrew Strathern and Pamela J. Stewart*

This compactly written book deals with how seniors, female and male, manage and enjoy their lives in the town of Kawanehonchō, Shizuoka Prefecture, Japan. Tanaka, one of the two authors, herself came from a small rural area, and seems naturalistically to have known how to carry out the fieldwork which forms the experiential basis for the book.

The study has a two-fold methodological approach. One is to give a quantitative conspectus of the structural picture, how the township is served by municipal agencies, what resources there are for the seniors in the community and what informal networks of support exist. The largely positive findings from the fieldwork are notable, given that the town was first established only in 2005, following an amalgamation of two former local towns. Remarkably, they seem to have fused well, at least in terms of welfare services for senior residents. At the outset of their book, Tanaka and Johnson deploy the concept of social capital as a way of assessing quality of life. Social capital refers to resources that people can look to for help with circumstances of their lives. Such capital can be, the authors note, either horizontal in character or hierarchical. The former refers to relatively egalitarian relationships, based on kinship or locality, and the latter on structures of government or administrative authority.

Horizontal social capital is perhaps the most significant resource for people, but the authors note that town authorities also provide a wide range of supporting services, public transport for access to services and events, managers who help plan happenings and assist in making participants feel at ease, and also volunteers who give unpaid help to seniors.

Managers help participants to feel they have *ikigai*, 'the purpose of life.' Events take place in small settings. Festivals are organized in honor of a local deity. Participants in events practice crafts at salon meetings. Joking and laughter contribute to senses of well-being. After events, organizers supply sweet foods and serve green tea harvested from local farms, creating a sense of pride in it as a product. An important feature of the area is that it is quite rural and there is enough land for residents to grow a range of vegetables and, importantly, giving them something to share with one another. Networks of informal reciprocity are created, and it is a part of the genius of social life in Kawanehonchō that there is a term for this, *otagaisama*, 'being in the same boat.' Men like to develop these networks via participation in games of quoits and ground golf, less taxing than full-scale golf courses. At some sites, a hot spring is nearby and is a favorite amenity. Seniors are taught exercises by managers, and the authors did not observe any obese people. Medical services are made available without charge. People are encouraged to stay in touch with one another by special local telephones, and these phones can be used free of charge. People need not feel lonely or neglected. Neighborly behavior is the norm. Another norm is to help people feel sumiyo, 'comfortable.'

Kawanehonchō residents realize that they live in a 'welfare town' designed for seniors who are retired and still need to have *ikigai*. As the residents themselves note, what is missing is a cohort of younger people. Young people like to go out to cities for employment and urban lifestyles. Counterbalancing to some extent this migratory outflow there is a flow of adults who like to come back and live a 'slower life,' one not so rushed by the imperatives of bigger cities.

Kawanehonchō serves as a useful potential model for other parts of the world, for example the USA. The authors themselves draw attention to this possibility. Reading this admirably perceptive study, however, brings to mind how much of all this depends on local ecology and history, and even more, in the last analysis, on that pervasive element, 'Japanese culture.'

We applaud this excellent, factual, thoughtful, and timely study for a world in which the needs of its seniors are becoming more evident as average life spans increase. Over this situation, however, falls a dark shadow, the global threat of the coronavirus (2019–2021). The authors take note of this, recognizing that for the future the conditions in which seniors can flourish in Kawanehonchō and throughout the world are potentially threatened. Anthropologists have long noted with regret the passing of 'traditional' cultures. Now we may be facing a threat to core features of cultures in general on a global scale unless the virus can be brought under control.

Birch Research Unit
Remote Learning Network,
February 2021
PJS and AJS

Note

(*) Pamela J. Stewart (Strathern) and Andrew J. Strathern are a wife-and-husband research team who are based in the Department of Anthropology, University of Pittsburgh, and co-direct the Cromie Burn Research Unit. They are frequently invited international lecturers and have worked with numbers of museums to assist them with their collections. Stewart and Strathern have published over 50 books; 80+ Prefaces for books; and over 200 articles, book chapters, and essays on their research in the Pacific (mainly Papua New Guinea and the South-West Pacific region, e.g., Samoa and Fiji); Asia (mainly Taiwan, and also including Mainland China and Inner Mongolia, and Japan); and Europe (primarily Scotland, Ireland, Germany and the European Union countries in general); and also New Zealand and Australia. Their most recent co-authored books include *Witchcraft, Sorcery, Rumors, and Gossip* (Cambridge University Press, 2004); *Kinship in Action: Self and Group* (Routledge Publishing, 2016, originally published 2011); *Peace-Making and the Imagination: Papua New Guinea Perspectives* (University of Queensland Press with Penguin Australia, 2011); *Ritual: Key Concepts in Religion* (Bloomsbury Academic Publications, 2014); *Working in the Field: Anthropological Experiences Across the World* (Palgrave Macmillan, 2014); *Breaking the Frames: Anthropological Conundrums* (Palgrave Macmillan, 2017); *Diaspora, Disasters, and the Cosmos: Rituals and Images* (Carolina Academic Press, 2018); *Sustainability, Conservation, and Creativity: Ethnographic Learning from Small-scale Practices* (Routledge Publishing, 2019); *Language* *and Culture in Dialogue* (Bloomsbury Academic Publishing, 2019); *Sacred Revenge in Oceania* (Cambridge University Press, 2019) and *Heritage, Ritual, Tradition and Contestation* (Carolina Academic Press, 2021, forthcoming).

Their recent co-edited books include *Research Companion to Anthropology* (Routledge Publishing, (2016, originally published 2015); *Exchange and Sacrifice* (Carolina Academic Press, 2008); and *Religious and Ritual Change: Cosmologies and Histories* (Carolina Academic Press, 2009); and the Updated and Revised Chinese version: Taipei, Taiwan: Linking Publishing, 2010; *Dealing with Disasters—Perspectives from Eco-Cosmologies* [along with Diana Riboli and Davide Torri] (Palgrave Macmillan, 2020); and *The Palgrave Handbook of Anthropological Ritual Studies* (Palgrave Macmillan, under contract and submitted [2021]).

Stewart and Strathern's current research includes the topics of Eco-Cosmological Landscapes; Ritual Studies; Political Peace-Making; Comparative Anthropological Studies of Disasters and Climatic Change; Language, Culture and Cognitive Science; and Scottish and Irish Studies. For many years they served as Associate Editor and General Editor (respectively) for the *Association for Social Anthropology in Oceania* book series and they are Co-Series Editors for the *Anthropology and Cultural History in Asia and the Indo-Pacific* book series. They also currently co-edit four book series: *Ritual Studies, Medical Anthropology, European Anthropology*, and *Disaster Anthropology*, and they are the long-standing Co-Editors of the Journal of Ritual Studies [Facebook: https://www.facebook.com/ritualstudies]. Their webpages, listing publications and other scholarly activities, are: http:// www.pitt. edu/~strather/ and http://www.StewartStrathern.pitt.edu/.

An extended Biographical Sketch can be found at https://cap-press.com/ pdf/9781611633986.pdf.

Acknowledgments

The authors want to thank their sources of professional and social support, without which this book could not have been written.

First, we thank the series editors, Andrew Strathern and Pamela Stewart, and the people at Carolina Academic Press, including Ryland Bowman and Susan Trimble, who made it possible for us to publish this work.

When Dr. Tanaka was a graduate student, she read "The Practice of Concern," by John W. Traphagan and hoped to publish a book on Japanese culture in the same series with his publisher. Her goal has now been reached.

We are grateful to Dr. Tanaka's employer, James Madison University, for a 2015 Department Summer Research Grant and the 2016 College of Liberal Arts Leave Program that funded her costs in travelling to, and collecting data in Kawanehonchō, Japan. Special salutes go to Mayor Toshio Suzuki and to the staff of the Kawanehonchō municipal welfare office and Kawanehonchō Council of Social Welfare (KCSW). The staff welcomed her with kindness to observe their facilities and provided resources to help her learn more about the programs. We appreciate the warm welcome and generous support extended to Dr. Tanaka by the residents of Kawanehonchō, too numerous to name. They kindly introduced her to key informants and took her for trips around the town and its suburbs. It helped us to understand why people move back to Kawanehonchō or move there for the first time.

While much of the data were collected on site by Dr. Tanaka, our study benefited from our access to secondary data. We gratefully acknowledge the Shizuokaken Sogō Kenkō Center for providing data through the Kawanehonchō municipal welfare office and the Mitsubishi Research Institute, Inc., for data through the Social Science Data Archive at the University of Tokyo.

Kimiko Tanaka thanks her daughters (Hillary Keiko and Irene Toshie, who were ages six and one at the beginning of this six year project), her spouse (Jamison Toshio Arimoto), her parents (Toshio and Keiko Tanaka), Mihoko Konishi (her grandmother), and Masako Tatebayashi (her great-aunt). Their continuous encouragement and support helped her balance her life as a mother and scholar. In addition, she thanks Nan E. Johnson for over 15 years of mentorship and friendship. At their first meeting at Michigan State University, she told Dr. Johnson of her goal of publishing a book about Japan. We are honored that we could work together to reach that goal.

Nan E. Johnson has previously studied the health status and health care received by older adults in the rural United States. She thanks Kimiko Tanaka for the opportunity to learn about elderly people in rural Japan through their collaboration on this book. Finally, Dr. Johnson appreciates having access to an office and other research supports at Michigan State University.

Introduction

In 1900, only 14 percent of the world's population lived in urban places, but it increased to an estimated 56 percent (4.4 billion) by 2020 (Kinsella 2001; United Nations 2014; Satterthwaite 2020). Since World War Two, the pace of urbanization has increased in the developing world due to net rural-to-urban migration and is now faster than in the developed world. Even so, the percentage of the elderly population is greater in rural than in urban areas in both the lesser developed and the more developed nations of the world (Kinsella 2001). Such a skewed age structure caused by net outmigration of young people to urban areas in search of opportunities for education and jobs has led to the stagnation of small and medium-sized towns (Kinsella 2001).

The rural elderly are vulnerable in both health status and access to healthcare services (Elnitsky and Alexy 1998; Kumar et al. 2001). In geographically isolated rural communities, low-density and dispersed populations created problems for the elderly in regards to service provision, personal mobility, and maintaining social connections (Walsh et al. 2012). In addition to geographical barriers and poorer access to health and emergency services, in comparison to urban seniors, rural seniors are considered disadvantaged in regards to having lower incomes and less education (Bacsu et al. 2014; Kumar et al. 2001). However, such disadvantages and vulnerabilities do not necessarily lead to negative health outcomes for the elderly living in rural areas.

As this book shows, words such as "rural" and "depopulation" do not simply equate with negative outcomes for the elderly. Some studies in the U.S. pointed out that negative health outcomes for the elderly living in rural areas are due to low socioeconomic status, poverty, and a lack of access to better health care. This book will illustrate that the social quality of a community at the micro and macro levels can buffer the negative effects of rurality on the well-being of the elderly. Critics have shown that the diversity among rural towns and villages, as created by environmental and industrial differences, makes it impossible for all of them to be uniformly compared to urban cities (Davis et al. 2012; Miller, Stokes, and Clifford 1987). As Davis et al. (2012) wrote: "Myths and stereotypes are often founded on small fragments of truth. Ageing in rural communities is subjected to many such myths that underpin some of the understandings held about rural living" (344). Despite the tendency of people to assume that rural communities are homogeneous, traditional, and faced with the challenges of net outmigration to cities, each rural town seeks its own way of revitalization and of support to the healthy living of the elderly. Due to particularities of geography, culture, and history, outcomes of dramatic population changes throughout the post-Second World War era are different for each locale, and how each municipal government implements policies is strongly influenced by local values and history (Matanle and Rausch 2011). Statistics are important in capturing patterns and successes of policies at the macro (supra-individual) level; but to understand successful aging in rural communities, it is crucial to conduct case studies at the micro (individual) level with qualitative methods to obtain self-reports from the elders in a vibrant rural community. Through understanding complexity and particularity of the locale, we aim to provide comparative and global understanding of rural aging.

Kawanehonchō in Shizuoka Prefecture, Japan, is such a community. Based on its significant population decrease and aging, the national government in Tokyo considered this town to be "endangered." "Rural" is often stereotyped as remote, poor, and depopulated. Kawanehonchō is located in a remote area, where 90 percent of the land is forested. There are no hospitals offering tertiary care, and no one would expect Kawanehonchō to have one of the longest healthy life expectancies in Japan and in the world (for further discussion, see Chapter 2). Kawanehonchō highlights the importance of the social quality of the community in achieving healthy aging, regardless of socioeconomic status, geographical remoteness, and lack of advanced medical technology.

In comparison to other rural communities studied in the United States (see Brown and Glasgow 2008), this study uses observations, face-to-face interviews, and surveys to find how elderly people in a rural community in Japan (Kawanehonchō) age successfully. The findings are important for other nations and communities, since aging and rural depopulation are global demographic trends. As the U.S. is aging rapidly, and as there are ever-increasing numbers of rural elderly people wishing to "age in place," this book will give a comparative example of the importance of community to healthy aging. Programs the research sites offer for the elderly provide applicable examples to promote healthy aging in rural areas of other nations. The findings will provoke discussions on the roles of population aging, rural sociology, and community development.

Finally, in understanding rural aging, it is also important look at issues of migration. What could motivate older rural adults to decide not to migrate (i.e., to age in place) or else to migrate to another rural county rather than to an urban county? Facing the relatively greater dearth of medical care in rural (than urban) America, older rural adults might choose to age in place if they can avail themselves of telehealth, "the use of telecommunications and computer technologies to make a broad spectrum of health-related services and information available to populations with limited access" (Grigsby and Goetz, 2004, 237). Because of the ongoing closures of rural hospitals in the U.S., access to face-to-face consultations with local physicians who can prescribe medications and interpret X-rays are becoming more limited. A nurse practitioner or a physician's assistant at a rural health clinic can provide simple primary care and contact an urban physician to prescribe medications. If the rural county can afford broadband internet service, then a local medical clinic can make and transmit an X-ray electronically to an urban hospital having a radiologist who can interpret the results. This study addresses why the elderly continue to stay in Kawanehonchō despite a lack of advanced hospitals and the possibility of migration in repopulating the rural depopulated towns in Japan.

Population aging and rural depopulation are serious problems especially for such Asian nations as Japan and South Korea, as well as for European nations such as Germany, Austria, Spain, Italy, and Greece (Hewitt 2004). Studies predict a decrease in Europe's rural population from 100 million to 75 million from 2000 to 2030. However, they also predict that the proportion of older people in rural places will grow due to out-migration of the young and in-migration of retirees (Burholt and Dobbs 2012; Baernholdt et al. 2012). This question is equally important to other nations including the U.S., Australia, and China, where studies found rural-urban disparities in health characteristics (Blazer et al. 1995; Ziersch et al. 2009; Norstrand and Xu 2012; McLaughlin, Stokes, and Nonoyama 2001; Elnitsky and Alexy 1998; Bacsu et al. 2014). The aging of the Baby Boomers (born in 1946–64) in the U.S. has raised various political debates in regards to the ability of continuing to pay for Social Security and Medicare at current benefit levels, to the lack of professional caregivers, and to the heavy family burden in providing care for the elderly (Pillemer and Glasgow 2000). The findings of our study will be important for other nations and communities, since aging and rural depopulation are global demographic trends (Kinsella 2001). Because Japan has one of the highest life expectancies in the world, it provides a natural laboratory in which to pursue answers to our research questions.

The plan of the book is as follows: In Chapter 1, we describe how rural Japan has changed socially and demographically. We explain how rural depopulation has led to political consolidation, and how the welfare system in Japan is placing more responsibility and autonomy on the municipalities. Some rural towns in Japan, such as Kawanehonchō, are actively responding to the demographic challenges initiated by municipal governments that have the advantage of developing unique programs reflecting the voices of local residents. Chapter 2 describes Kawanehonchō, explains how it became a rural depopulated town, and discusses why the town provides an important example to understand and discuss rural aging comparatively. In Chapter 3, we review theoretical frameworks (collective efficacy theory and social capital) to understand the inseparability of successful aging from the quality of neighborhoods and communities. We explain our research methods in Chapter 4. In Chapter 5, we examine Kawanehonchō with secondary data. Chapter 6 summarizes the findings based on observations of activities provided for the elderly in this town, and Chapter 7 sheds light on rural aging through the eyes and words of its leaders. Chapter 8 presents our findings from our survey of elders participating in two community programs developed locally and specifically for them. Finally, in Chapter 9, we discuss the possibility of net inmigration of older adults to Kawanehonchō, and Chapter 10 includes discussions on challenges in rural depopulation and healthy aging.

Successful Aging in a Rural Community in Japan

One

Rural Japan

Facing Demographic Challenges

The Meiji Restoration in 1868 was one of the decisive events that brought significant social change to Japanese society. Japan shifted from a traditional feudal country with isolationist policies to one open to modernization and economically competitive with Western colonial powers. The Meiji Civil Code in 1898 codified the *ie* system, the family line of succession passing primarily through male primogeniture[1] (Tanaka and Iwasawa 2010; Tanaka and Johnson 2008). Under the *ie* system, children were required to unconditionally obey their parents. The relationship between father and son, like that between subject and ruler, strengthened national patriotism. Such a vertical hierarchy of families formed the ideological basis for the family-state concept, that the state is a single family with the Emperor as its head. It prioritizes the authority of the family and the state over individual freedom (Tanaka and Johnson 2008; Ishida 1971; Asai and Kameoka 2005).

Under the *ie* system, while second-born and later-born sons were relatively free to move to urban areas to work after they left school around age 15, the eldest sons were expected to remain or to return as a successor to take care of the family (Palmer 1988). Ensuring the survival of at least one son as a successor encouraged families to have more than one child. As modernization contributed to lower infant mortality, the government discussed how to provide stable jobs for excess labor on farms (Imai 1970). Some later-born sons moved to urban areas of Japan, and some moved to foreign nations, such as the United States and Brazil, to seek a better life. In other words, the need for subsequent sons to leave the household became a strong "push" factor; at the same time, the increased need for labor due to rapid industrialization and urbanization became a "pull" factor of migration (Tan 2006). The *ie* system that emphasized familial succession also contributed to maintaining the number of farmers overall with regional variations from the beginning of the Meiji period to the middle of the 20th century (Noda 2012; Tama 2014; Sakane 2011).

It was during the economic development after the Second World War when rural depopulation became visible. When Emperor Meiji replaced the old feudal system of the Tokugawa shoguns in 1868, Japan was a predominantly agricultural society. About 70 percent of the population were engaged in agriculture in the mid-1880s, contributing to over 40 percent of the gross national product (Tomlinson 1995). While more than 80 percent of the Japanese population lived in rural areas in 1920, by the late 1950s, the urban population exceeded the rural population, and in the late 1970s, about three-fourths of the population lived in cities (K. Tsutsumi 2011). Due to continous outmigration of the young, the proportion of the elderly age 65 and above engaged primarily in farming had increased from 64.9 percent in 2015 to 69.6 percent in 2020 while the overall number of farmers primarily engaged in farming decreased from 1.757 million to 1.363 million (Ministry of Agriculture, Forestry and Fisheries 2020).

After the Second World War, the democratization policy denied the legality of the old family system. In the revised Civil Code of 1947, the exclusive inheritance by the eldest son was abolished, and the inheritance of family property was changed from primogeniture to the equal inheritance of all children, and marriage became based on the mutual agreement of two people (Matsubara 1969). Before World War II, education for women was to become a *"Ryōsai Kenbo"* (good wife, clever mother). The educational reform under the U.S. Occupation Army consciously improved women's status by drastically expanding equal educational opportunities for women (Narumiya 1986). The number of "love matches" began outnumbering arranged marriages, and marriage began to take place more frequently in urban regions where a larger proportion of young people reside than in rural areas where traditional norms persist strongly despite the legal abolition of the *ie* system (Kumagai 2008). Negative images including job insecurity, the demanding physical labor of farming, and the difficulty of attracting brides led to more male high school graduates leaving their towns for college and job opportunities and remaining in urban areas as these jobs provided greater safety and promotion. Lack of successors to the family farms resulted in increased numbers of elderly people living alone in rural areas (Onishi 2011), increasing the proportion of never-married men in rural depopulated areas (Tanaka and Iwasawa 2010), and such a trend poses great threats to the landscape, ecosystem, and the rural community (Su, Okanishi, and Chen 2018). With the liberation of the agricultural market and the competitive global market, the farming population faces the challenge of not only losing successors, but also losing the protection from the government (Sugimoto 2014, 72).

Causes and Consequences of Dramatic Postwar Fertility Decline

The Total Fertility Rate (TFR) is an often-used demographic measure referring to the average number of children per woman if all women lived to the end of their childbearing years and bore children according to the age-specific fertility rates observed in a given calendar year (te Velde et al. 2012). The Japanese TFR was 2.14 at the beginning of the 1970s (Figure 1.1). At this point, the Japanese government was concerned with the possibility of over-population and held symposiums that emphasized the optimum number of children to be a maximum of two children per woman (Kito 2011, 27). Strongly influenced by the Western idea of liberal democracy after the Second World War, and accompanied by urbanization and industrialization, women liberated from traditional gender norms postponed marriage and childbirth (Atoh 2008). As women gained higher education, the meaning of a good marriage no longer referred to being an obedient full-time caretaker of family members and producing offspring for the spouse's family. Consequently, the age at first marriage rose from 23 to 29.4 years for women and 27 to 31.1 years for men between 1910 and 2018, and the age gap between the husband and the wife shrank from 4 years in 1910 to 1.7 years in 2018 (National Institute of Population and Social Security Research 2020).

In Japan, the average age at a woman's first birth increased from 26.1 years to 30.2 years from 1980 to 2018 (National Institute of Population and Social Security Research 2020). The trends toward later and fewer marriages are similar across most industrial societies. However, unlike in other industrial nations, these trends have not been attended by large increases in births outside marriage in Japan. In other words, the current trend of declined fertility rates in Japan is a more direct result of the postponement of the marriage than in other nations (Raymo 2003). The average proportion of people who have never married between age groups 45–49 and 50–54 increased from 1.7 percent for men and 3.3 percent for women in 1970 to 23.4 percent for men and 14.1 percent for women in 2015. Without any changes in the trend of Japanese people postponing marriage, this rate is expected to increase to 29.5 percent for men and 18.7 percent for women by 2040 (Cabinet Office Japan 2020). Yasunori Yoshimura, a professor emeritus at Keio University School of Medicine, says that women today are reluctant to have children due to a lack of support for mothers to continue working. Yoshimura says it is called "social infertility," the environment that makes it harder for people to get married, conceive, and have children (Ito 2015).

Today, Japan has become one of the nations with extremely low fertility rates (Figure 1.1). While the U.S. and France have sustained a rate of around two children per woman by menopause since the mid-1970s, the Japanese TFR has fallen much below the replacement-level, meaning that Japanese fertility is below the level necessary for a population to reproduce itself (Livingston 2019). Within a decade, the Japanese government has shifted the policy from reducing to increasing fertility rates. Since the early 1990s, the Japanese government has implemented parental leave policies and childcare services. However, these policies have been criticized for the failure to support all women regardless of their income or education (Goldstein, Sabotka, and Jasilioniene 2009). Although the number of childcare centers has increased, the demand for childcare services is growing faster than the supply. It has resulted in a shortage of childcare services especially in large metropolitan areas (United Nations 2015). Despite these efforts, the failure of these policies to alleviate the strain on working mothers is reflected in Japan's ranking second from the bottom of 18 members of the Organization for Economic Co-operation and Development (OECD) in terms of coverage and strength of policies for work-family reconciliations and family-friendly work arrangements (United Nations 2015).

According to the report published by the United Nations Development Programme (UNDP), Japan ranks 23rd out of 162 countries in the 2018

Figure 1.1 Total Fertility Rates of Japan, the U.S. and France 1950–2016

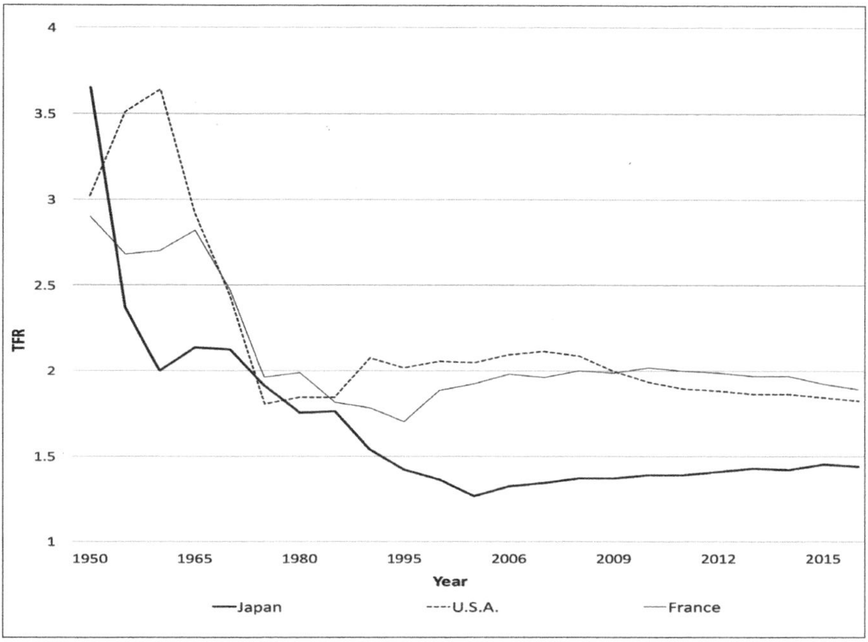

Source: National Institute of Population and Social Security Research

Gender Inequality Index (GII), a measurement reflecting gender-based in-equalities in reproductive health, empowerment, and economic activity. In comparison, the U.S ranked 42nd and South Korea ranked 10th. While Japanese women who reached at least a secondary level of education exceeded that of men (95.2 percent vs. 92.2 percent), Japanese women only hold 13.7 percent of parliamentary seats (United Nations Development Programme 2019). According to the White Paper on Gender Equality 2017, female employment rates are increasing in every prefecture; but the proportion of managerial positions held by women remains at a low level (13 percent). This percentage is significantly lower than in Western nations such as the United States (43.4 percent) and Sweden (39.2 percent) and in Asian nations such as Singapore (34.2 percent) and the Philippines (46.6 percent) (Cabinet Office Japan 2017).

It is often discussed on the news that women with full-time jobs continue to face discrimination by being demoted at work by the "kind consideration" of the company for moving women with children to less stressful sections that enable them to balance work and family responsibilities. The 2017 White Paper on Gender Equality shows that about 80 percent of Japanese men in double-income families do not contribute to the housework. When it comes to childcare, about 70 percent of Japanese men do not participate regardless of their wives' employment status (Cabinet Office Japan 2017). As a result, Japanese women, especially with careers, are hesitant to marry and become a mother since the cost of marriage and childbearing is too high in a society where the great responsibility of the care of family members lies heavily upon married women. Such cost is especially high for women marrying young male farmers living in rural areas. The media calls such situations of bachelor farmers facing a scarcity of potential brides, "bride drought" or "bride famine" (Knight 2003).

Greatly influenced by the postwar fertility decline, the population of Japan gradually started to decline since 2007 (Figure 1.2). The decline in the fertility rates also accelerated population aging. In 1985, the proportion of Japanese people ages 65 years or more exceeded 10 percent, although Sweden. France, Germany, Italy, and the U.S. all exceeded 10 percent earlier than Japan. However, in 2015, this percentage had increased to 26.6 percent in Japan, exceeding all of these other nations and suggesting a more rapid pace of population aging in Japan compared to Western nations (Statistic Bureau of Japan 2019). By contrast, the share of the young population (aged under 15 years) fell from 35.4 percent in 1950 to 13.1 percent in 2010, and is expected to shrink to 9.1 percent by 2060 (Hara 2015). Figure 1.3 illustrates such dramatic change in population age structure caused by below-replacement fertility and rising longevity.

Figure 1.2 Population Change of Japan 1872–2065

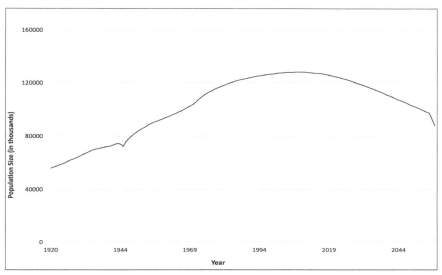

Source: National Institute of Population and Social Security Research

Figure 1.3 Population Change in Japan by Age Composition 1884–2012

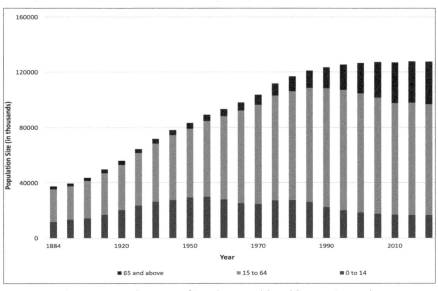

Source: National Institute of Population and Social Security Research

Understanding Rural Aging through "seken"

Historically, especially in Japan's rural areas, harmonious social integration—the view that people should care for each other beyond the family—has been a highly valued form of social capital. Such emphasis is reflected in the characterization of Japanese culture as collective as opposed to individualistic (Traphagan 2004; Sugimoto 2014). Particularly rural areas hold stronger traditional norms of filial piety that require family members to take care of their parents. *Seken* is one of the key concepts to understanding rural culture in Japan. *Seken* translates as "world," "society," and "public" in English. However, it is more than what these translations imply (Abe 1995; Koukami 2006; Sugimoto 2014; Kashimura 2013). Whereas the society represents a group composed of distinct individuals and defined in explicit terms such as race and nationality, *seken* is holistic and implies some unknowable range of social networks that link individuals (Kitayama and Imada 2008, 177). Sugimoto (2014) defined *seken* as "an imagined community that has the normative power of approving or disapproving of and sanctioning individual behavior" (335). Abe (1995) considers this concept a key to understanding Japanese patterns of social behavior. *Seken* strongly influences people's behaviors through defining whether their actions are deviant since it is almost impossible for most Japanese to conceive the meaning of the self without simultaneously considering how the self is regarded by the *seken*.

In rural areas, where traditional norms based on filial piety remain strong (Tanaka and Iwasawa 2010), the normative power of *seken* for family members to take care of their elders is also strong. Concerning the *seken*, rural Japanese may be hesitant to ask for public support for their elders (Takegawa 2012). However, such familial responsibility for elder care is a myth, as it is historically a new phenomenon for the Japanese elderly to live long enough to receive long duration of care from family members (Ueno 2013). As rural depopulation became a public issue discussed by government and featured in the media, the increase in the number of elderly people living alone and the decrease of three-generation households made the development of community-care options in rural areas to be increasingly urgent. Still, the rural elderly and their families tend to resist asking for extrafamilial support due to lack of familiarity in using public services and to the wish to observe filial piety (Takano 2009). Thus, rural municipal governments and elder care facilities face additional challenges to persuade younger relatives that cepting extrafamilial public support for the care of their elders is not shirking filial responsibility.

Government's Response to Rural Depopulation

In 1960, the proportion of the elderly did not differ greatly between rural areas depopulated by net outmigration and the nation as a whole (6.7 percent in depopulated rural areas vs. 5.7 percent as national average). However, this gap had increased by 1990 (18.7 percent vs. 12.1 percent) and widened even further by 2010 (32.8 percent vs. 23.0 percent) (Ministry of Internal Affairs and Communications 2015, 2016). Rural depopulation influenced the quality of elders' lives through a loss of accessible markets within walking distance, a loss of local transportation, and a decrease in the demand for buses and trains (Tanimoto 2012; Matanle and Sato 2010; Matanle and Rausch 2011). Since the 1970s, the Japanese government introduced policies to tackle the problems caused by rural depopulation.

The Depopulated Areas Emergency Measures Law (*Kaso chiiki taisaku kinkyū sochihō*) was enacted in 1970 and remained in effect for 10 years. It had these objectives: to support the independence of residents of depopulated areas financially through increasing employment opportunities, limiting regional wealth gaps, and preserving the landscape of the countryside (Feldhoff 2013; Assmann 2016; Matanle and Rausch 2011). To achieve these goals, the government provided subsidies to fund infrastructure for communication and transportation (Feldhoff 2013). Next, the 1980 Depopulated Areas Special Promotion Law (*Kaso chiiki shinkō tokubetsu sochihō*) was enacted to last until 1990 in order to improve rural life conditions through strengthening the transportation infrastructure. In 1990, this 1980 law was modified as a special revitalization law (*Kaso chiiki kasseika tokubetsuhō*) with great emphasis on 'soft' development i.e., the communal autonomy by creating local income and the promotion of communal development to accompany 'hard' development, such as infrastructure and public institutions (Feldhoff 2013; Matanle and Rausch 2011). In the past, these government policies heavily focused on 'hard' developments as nearly 50 percent of the funding was spent on transport, information, and communication infrastructure. Since the early 1990s, more emphasis has been placed upon 'soft' development (Feldhoff 2013).

In the 2000 Special Law Promoting Independence in Depopulated Areas (*Kaso chiiki jiritsu sokushin tokubetsu sochihō*), the term *kaso chiiki* was defined as depopulated rural areas that have experienced significant population decline that has weakened the vitality and infrastructures necessary for daily living (Feldhoff 2013; Matanle and Rausch 2011). About 52 percent of land areas fit the definition, and about 7.3 percent of the total population lived in *kaso chiiki* (Feldhoff 2013; Lützeler 2008).

In addition to providing funds to improve 'hard' and 'soft' developments, the government merged depopulated towns. As the proportion of the elderly people increased in depopulated areas, accompanied by lack of successors to maintain the land, various towns lost their ability to manage and were consolidated, merged or amalgamated into neighboring municipalities. It is estimated that, between 1994 and 2006, 60.8 percent of cities, towns, and villages took part in the Great Heisei Era Amalgamation Initiative (*Heisei no Dai Gappei*). This percentage increased to 70.3 percent when only considering cities, towns, and villages where the population was less than 10,000 (Odagiri 2014, 13). Kawanehonchō, our research site, was created in 2005 by merging two neighboring towns faced with dramatic depopulation (Hon-kawanechō and Naka-kawanechō).

In theory, municipalities should become more self-efficient and self-governing after the Great Heisei Era Amalgamation Initiative. However, such movement can negatively influence folk performance preservation, especially for amateur performers in depopulated communities due to already scarce resources competing with larger pools of practitioners (Thompson 2008; Rausch 2016). Such amalgamations took place in other nations such as Canada, the United Kingdom (U.K.), South Korea, and the United States (U.S.); but it could result in higher taxes, debts, and reduced opportunities for citizens to participate (Rausch 2016). In Japan, local residents also feared the amalgamation law could lead to the homogenization of residential neighborhoods and could weaken or erase local identities and distinctive cultural heritage (Traphagan and Thompson 2006; Matanle and Sato 2010). At the same time, local residents feared that their towns would become *genkai shūraku* (marginal communities), defined as communities with significant depopulation, a majority of residents at ages 65 and older, an inability to manage, and a threat of extinction. These limits can arise through the net outmigration of younger residents and the "aging in place" of older residents, both of which can result in more than half of the total population being ages 65 and over (Assmann 2016; Feldhoff 2013; Yamashita 2015). Yamashita (2015) considers *genkai shūraku* to be more the result of low fertility rates, which deplete communities of a critical mass of youths to sustain the communities in the future. As of 2006, there were 7,878 *genkai shūraku* in Japan (Assman 2016, xvi).

Greater Responsibility for Municipal Governments in Promoting Healthy Aging

The welfare system in Japan is changing by giving more responsibility and autonomy to the municipalities. In the past, the national government had been in charge of elderly welfare services, and everything had been centrally planned and administered through municipal governments and Social Welfare Corporations. Faced with a rapid, steep increase of the elderly in the 1990s, medical and long-term care systems were either established or reconstructed (Shimada et al. 2016). The 1990 amendment of the eight welfare-related laws and of the Social Welfare Services Law articulated the importance of community-oriented welfare and delegated the authority to municipal governments to decide the placement of local citizens who need social welfare services (Aratame 2007, 4).

The Social Welfare Law, revised in 2000, aimed to promote community-based welfare, and it identified the municipal Social Welfare Council to take a major role in promoting social welfare in the community. Public Long Term Care Insurance (LTCI), implemented in 2000, provided a framework to implement community-based welfare for the elderly. Under the LTCI system, the primary insured persons are those aged 65 and over (Category 1) and the subscribers of the health insurance whose ages are between 40 and 64 years old (Category II). The premium is collected through municipality and deducted from pensions for those belonging to Category I, and through an additional premium to be paid for health insurance for those who belong to Category II[2] (National Institute of Population and Social Security Research

2014). The LTCI system is classified into seven levels, depending on the cognitive, physical, and mental status. First two levels are classified as "requiring support levels 1 and 2" where individuals require partial assistance in daily living and they can access preventive care services in the LTCI system. The other five levels are those who cannot conduct daily activities without any assistance, and they are classified as "requiring care levels 1 to 5," level 5 being the most serious state (Akiyama et al. 2018). After the assessment, service users can choose comprehensive health, medical, and welfare services from agents (National Institute of Population and Social Security Research 2014; Akiyama et al. 2018).

LTCI is a mandatory social insurance plan that covers the elderly who were previously protected partly by the health insurance system and the welfare measures for the elderly. LTCI reflects the limitation of families in taking care of the elderly by themselves, as well as the financial limitations of the previous system that gave free healthcare to those who were over 70 years old (National Institute of Population and Social Security Research 2014). LTCI was not designed simply to provide care to the elderly who require long-term care, but its emphasis is on the importance of providing support for the independence of the elderly. In other words, LTCI promotes community care services including home help, day service, and short stays as a primary means for elder care, resulting in shifting the eldercare from the institution to the community and encouraging the elderly people to have self-reliant lives at home for as long as they can (Aratame 2007). It also aims to mitigate the unpaid family caregiver's burden as family caregivers can be released from some aspects of caregiving (Fu et al. 2017). LTCI benefits include a wide range of institutional as well as in-home benefits including housekeeping, personal care such as bathing services, nurse visits, and the costs for leasing assistive devices to perform Activities of Daily Living (ADLs) (Rhee, Done, and Anderson 2015). Finally, LTCI places a great emphasis on local welfare services to be creative and to take the initiative in providing the community care services. Municipalities are insurers and expect to deliver services in collaboration with the national government, prefectures, medical care insurers, and pension insurers (National Institute of Population and Social Security Research 2014).

Japan's healthcare policy includes both medical care insurance that applies to medical treatment due to illness, injury, preparation for hospitalization, surgery, outpatient visits, and LTCI that applies to people needing assistance with nursing care (Akiyama et al. 2018). In other words, an insured person over age 65 is eligible for both medical care insurance and LTCI. As population aging accelerates, both costs continue to increase. The total medical expenditure for medical care insurance reached US $458 billion (US $1 = JPY 80 in 2011), of which US $203 billion were spent on the elderly. The total expenditure for LTCI grew from US $45 billion to US $99 billion from 2000 to 2010 (Akiyama et al. 2018, 2). Looking at this issue globally, Japan's LTCI is considered generous: it covers a substantial portion of need for disability care (Chen et al. 2016). Japan is known for keeping the long-term care expenditure low (1.2 percent of GDP in 2010) compared with Sweden (3.58 percent) and the Netherlands (3.7 percent). Furthermore, Japan is one of the few OECD nations imposing the minimum of 130 hours of training to become an entry-level certified care worker compared with two weeks to become a home health aide in the U.S. (OECD 2013). In contrast to the American System, the Japanese government strictly regulates prices for medical treatments and pharmaceuticals; it allows the healthcare cost to be considerably lower than in the U.S. (Ikegami 1991). However, the rapid speed of aging in Japan challenges the sustainability of the system. Japanese public spending on LTCI is projected to more than double, even to reach 4.4 percent of GDP in 2050 (OECD 2013). Population aging in Japan will directly influence the sustainability of LTCI. In fact, in the first fifteen years of LTCI, all services were subjected to a 10 percent copayment. However, copayment for LTCI for high-income earners increased from 10 percent to 20 percent in 2015, and 20 percent to 30 percent in 2018 (Ministry of Health, Labour 2017).

Japan continues to face the problem of how to finance long-term care expenditures as the nation continues to age and as aging in place remains popular. Hence, the Japanese government pressures the municipalities to build a community-based integrated care system (*chiiki hōkatsu* care system). The integrated community care system, a scheme created by the Japanese government in 2005, places great responsibility on the regional (as opposed to the national) government to design, promote, and run community-based prevention programs for local senior citizens who are at risk of enrolling in LTCI. The recipients receive programs for health promotion, exercise, and social participation (Ricart 2014; National Institute of Population and Social Security Research 2014).

The concept of a community-based integrated care system is founded on the coordination between the formal health, welfare, and medical care specialists and the informal or mutual activities by residents, such as volunteers (Morikawa 2014, 4). Thus, this system is not just based on the coordination of formal services, for it emphasizes the involvement of various resources of local communities, including senior clubs, volunteers, and regional senior gatherings. Reliance on the integration of national, regional, and municipal systems is expected to increase as the LTCI shifts the care of responsibility for those not requiring support or care to the community-based integrated care system.

While the social welfare system is heavily pressured by ever-increasing numbers of the elderly, the informal caregivers have continued to be a major source of long-term care provision even after the LTCI system was implemented. Approximately 70 percent of the care recipients rely on family members as caregivers, and more than 60 percent of the elderly expect family members to support them in later life (Wakui et al. 2012; Cabinet Office Japan 2011). Thus, it is crucial for the elderly to remain healthy as long as possible to reduce the burden on their caregivers, as well as on their public-service requirements. For those who are not classified and for those who are classified at early stages of dependency (requiring support level 1 and 2), the municipal governments provide programs and services that emphasize prevention and social integration. Municipalities are given greater responsibility and autonomy (than national and regional organizations) in identifying local resources and providing programs and services to the elderly in Japan.

The Importance of Uniqueness in Understanding Rural Aging

Postwar urbanization and economic development have spread the idea that population increase equals development, and this idea makes it difficult to perceive economic improvement without population increase (Miyaguchi 2003). In rural communities, the demographic challenge of depopulation can be considered as an opportunity rather than a cause for despair. There is a movement for the people seeking a slower life to return to rural areas (Kousaka 2012; Odagiri 2014). Younger generations today also positively perceive local areas, and there is an emerging tendency to be actively involved in local networks (Kousaka 2012; Klien 2016). While there has been a trend of merging cities, towns, and villages for administrative reasons, there is now a movement to rediscover the uniqueness of rural regions and their social capital (Odagiri 2014). Rather than being solely directed by the government, rural depopulated towns today seek solutions in a grassroots manner. Listening to residents' diverse opinions and the involvement of local residents appear to be keys for the survival of depopulated towns today (Kitahara 1994; Odagiri 2014). Odagiri (2014) claims that it is necessary for municipal governments to fully involve their employees, employees of non-governmental organizations, and volunteers to address and discuss problems and solutions.

The demographic challenge of depopulation and aging made some rural people aging in place to be more successful than others. To understand rural aging in Japan, it is crucial to understand the uniqueness of programs, facilities, and activities that are inseparable from the geography, history, industry, and culture of each locality. Kamikatsuchō in Tokushima Prefecture is a successful story. The elderly grow herbs that are served with food at restaurants. A corporation named Irodori supported the elderly in providing information and training for marketing. It took Irodori and the elderly 30 years of trial and error to maximize its market share to be the top, with as much as 70 percent of herbs (garnishes) sold in Japan (Fujinami 2016). The success story of the elderly learning to be the engine of the revitalization of the town became a movie titled *It's a Beautiful Life—IRODORI* (Minorikawa 2012).

Takasuchō, a depopulated town in Hokkaido Prefecture, was rewarded by the national government for its successful attempts to revitalize the town through effective local programs (Kitahara 1994). They created a register to check the health status of the residents and to develop their own programs for people over 30 to get full medical checkups. Placing great emphasis on preventive health care contributed to the reduction of medical fees and a shorter duration for medical treatments (ibid). Sustaining access to healthcare is extremely important in repopulating villages (Nishikawa, Tsubokura, and Yamazaki 2016). After the Fukushima nuclear disaster, in March, 2011, Kawauchi Village in Fukushima, located near the nuclear power plant, was forced to evacuate. Among 2,746 residents, 1,820 returned to the village. Before the disaster, there was only one physician in the only national insurance clinic in this village who handled all the patients visiting the clinic. He transferred difficult cases to other hospitals. In responding to such problems, municipal governments collaborated with specialized doctors in the private sector to provide quality chronic care in the repopulated village after the disaster (ibid). This is a good example of the municipal government quickly responding to the needs of the local population and their wish to age in place even after the disaster.

Based on the survey of the elderly living alone in a depopulated town called Yazuchō in Tottori Prefecture, Takegawa (2012) reported that these elderly strongly wished to live in their local communities for the rest of their lives because they did not want to leave the town where they had built relationships with their neighbors. To prevent the elderly from getting out of the loop of human relations, the town placed great emphasis on managing the programs at the district level, an even smaller administrative units than a town. Such small-scale management enabled them to consider the uniqueness of each district and focus on issues specific to that district. Furthermore, it allowed local citizens to view issues more relatable to them in creating support networks (Takegawa 2012).

Nanmokumura in Gunma Prefecture is one of the villages and towns called *genkai shūraku* (marginal communities) discussed above, and 58.31 percent of the elderly are 65 and above (Aikawa 2016). About 40 percent of the elderly in this village are 75 and above, and the town has come to be known as the first town that might vanish. By visiting and talking with people in this town, Aikawa (2016) discovered that people in the town were not pessimistic, as he had found them described in the news media. He saw people in their 80s and 90s enjoying growing their own vegetables on their small farms. He perceived the village as a longevity village, not just the next village to disappear. The village is located in a remote area so that residents are not worried about merger with other towns which are geographically distant. One of the residents, who is in his 70s, responded that the village is proud of having active elderly who engage in agriculture. He criticizes the shallow, negative reporting about the village by the media, which he thinks are basing their stories of Nanmokumura on unfounded biases against elderly people (ibid). To fully understand depopulation and rural aging, visiting the actual sites, observing, and interacting with the local people are crucial to gain a rich understanding based on the unique local contexts.

Summary

In this chapter, we have described the demographic trends in Japan since the Second World War that have resulted in rural-urban net migration of young adults who have left behind their elders, who often live alone. Aware of the emerging need for extrafamilial sources of eldercare, especially in rural areas, it became crucial to give roles to municipal governments and non-governmental organizations in tackling the issues. In the next chapter, we shall describe the social and economic history of Kawanehonchō, the town that is the case study for this book. If eldercare programs initiated by the municipal and non-governmental organizations are to succeed in any rural community in Japan, the success ought to be readily found in Kawanehonchō. The town continues to face serious depopulation while the local elderly continue to achieve healthy aging.

∾ Two ∾

Kawanehonchō

Structural Support for Rural Aging

Previously, we discussed the three great demographic transitions, fertility, mortality, and rural-to-urban migration in Japan after the Second World War. To repeat: national death and birth rates have declined. The decline in the death rate suggests that the actual *number* of people living in rural areas and surviving to old age has risen. The decline in the birth rate, exacerbated by the net rural-urban migration, has meant that the *percentage* of the rural population that is elderly has also been rising. In rural Japan, a major result of these demographic trends is that most of the rural elderly cannot solely expect that they will have junior relatives nearby on whom to depend for hands-on care. The situation creates a cultural crisis especially for the rural elderly in Japan. The *ie* system was abolished by the Civil Code Reform after the Second World War, but it continues to influence Japanese families (see Chapter 1). The *ie* system holds the married eldest son responsible for caring for his parents and eventually inheriting the family house (Kato 2013). Unlike its American counterpart, the *ie* system presumes the presence of his wife co-residing with or near his parents in order to give practical support to them in their old age.

However, the solutions to this cultural and demographic crisis in rural Japan should also be relevant to rural elderly in other nations. For instance, elderly Americans have been seeing an increase in their numbers and percentages, especially in the rural retirement counties studied by Brown and

Glasgow (2008). According to the U.S. census, 17.5 percent of the rural population was elderly in comparison to 13.8 percent in urban areas during the 2012 to 2016 period. Rural areas are expected to gain more elderly, as the population 65 years and older is projected to reach 80.8 million by 2040 (Symens and Trevelyan 2019). In Malaysia, the rural-urban migration of young adults resulted in a greater proportion of rural elderly Malays expecting to face issues due to insufficient and unsatisfactory programs (Shahar, Earland, and Abd Rahman 2001). In Spain, where the primary responsibility for care has traditionally been on spouses and daughters, insufficient development of public services has resulted in a "crisis of care," referring to the unsustainability of the traditional model of care that ties women to the domestic sphere even as the labor force participation of women increases (Elizalde-San Miguel and Díaz-Gandasegui 2016). Therefore, our two purposes in this chapter are (1) to describe the rural town of Kawanehonchō, Japan, and explain why it is an ideal place to study, and (2) to describe what the public and private sectors are doing to address the cultural and demographic crisis.

Kawanehonchō: An Attractive Rural Town for Elderly People to Age in Place

Two neighboring rural towns, Honkawanechō and Nakakawanechō, went through dramatic depopulation and population aging after the Second World War. The economy of the towns was heavily agricultural: the production of charcoal and forest products was important, along with the cultivation of shiitake mushrooms and green tea. The heavy focus on agriculture caused the outmigration to urban areas of young men and women. As a result, the combined populations of Honkawanechō and Nakakawanechō shrank by more than 50 percent (from 16,919 to 7,192) from 1965 to 2015. For fiscal reasons caused by depopulation, these two towns were merged in 2005 to form the City of Kawanehonchō, outlined on the map (Figure 2.1).

Figure 2.1 Geographic Location of Kawanehonchō, Japan

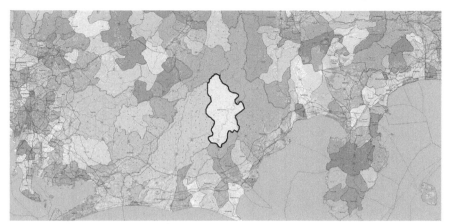

Source: Map of Kawanehonchō created using Mapline.

Despite the depopulation of Kawanehonchō from 1965 to 2015, the number of households remained steady (Figure 2.2). To understand why the number of households remained steady, consider the age-specific population counts over the 50 years (Figure 2.3). The greatest population decline was for people aged 15–64, the prime ages for going away to get educational degrees and jobs elsewhere. There was also a noticeable decline of people under age 15 years, probably because the outmigration of young adults carried their births away from Kawanehonchō to be born or counted elsewhere. By contrast, the population aged 65 and older increased (Figure 2.3). According to the Kawanehonchō municipal website, the average number of people per household shrank from close to five in 1965 to fewer than three in 2015 (Kawanehonchō Office 2018).

Figure 2.2 Population Change in Kawanehonchō by Sex

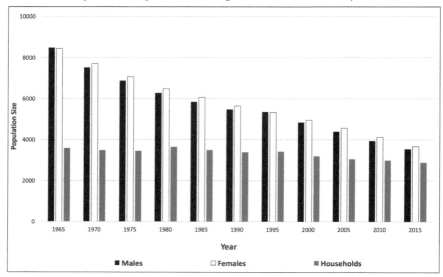

Source: Kawanehonchō Municipal Website based on censuses (Kawanehonchō Office 2018).
Note: Prior to 2005, data from Honkawanechō and Nakakawanechō are combined to calculate
the number of males, females, and households.

Figure 2.3 Population Change in Kawanehonchō by Age Composition

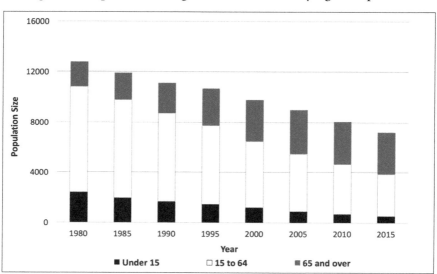

Source: Census Japan

Green tea has been the major crop in the area since the late 16th century. After the Meiji Era (1868–1912), green tea production increased and Kawane green tea became famous in Japan for its high quality (Fukase 2008). Tea leaves are mechanically harvested in the United States. However, since the tea trees in Kawanehonchō grow on steep mountain slopes (Figure 2.4) where heavy machines can easily roll over, harvesting Kawane green tea leaves requires manual labor. In the past, Japanese women temporarily migrated to Kawanehonchō to hand-pick the tea leaves (Matsumoto 2009). Before the Second World War, close to 50 percent of green tea was processed fully by manual labor versus 10 percent in other areas (Kawanehonchō Office 2008). However, since the late 1970s, it has become increasingly hard to find women to harvest the tea, and increasingly, the labor gap is being filled by the usage of mechanical harvesters (Fukase 2008).

Figure 2.4 Scenery from Kawanehonchō

Photo provided by Yasuro Ozawa

Another source of revenue is tourism. The commercial leaders of Kawanehonchō have successfully promoted the area as a vacation site. Newspaper articles and television programs have lured families of all ages and levels of physical ability to the area not only to enjoy beautiful views of mountains, rivers, and forests, but also to enjoy green tea, star-gazing, heritage train rides, hot springs, fishing, camping, canoeing, hiking, and hanggliding. Hikers can view a turquoise blue lake from the 90-meters-long famous suspension bridge called Yume no Tsuribashi (Dream Suspension Bridge), ranked by TripAdvisor as one of the top 10 bridges to visit in a lifetime (Konuma 2019) (Figure 2.5). For children and their parents, the steam locomotives have been renovated to look like the characters in the TV series "Thomas the Tank Engine" (Figure 2.6). The locomotives transport the riders over the river and through woods and tunnels. The popularity of the train rides in summer makes it difficult to purchase tickets. The Oku-Ōi Kojō Station is an unstaffed station located in the middle of Nagashima Dam Lake (Figure 2.7).

Figure 2.5 Yume no Tsuribashi (Dream Suspension Bridge in Kawanehonchō)

Photo provided by Yoshihito Ōishi

Figure 2.6 Thomas the Tank Engine in Kawanehonchō

Photo provided by Yasuro Ozawa

Figure 2.7 Oku-Ōi Kojō Station

Photo provided by Toshio Tanaka

Furthermore, recent news on the public and social media consider Kawanehonchō to be the town of healthy aging. With regard to healthy life expectancy (called *otasshado* in Japanese), the average number of disability-free years of life expectable for someone on his or her sixty-fifth birthday was calculated from the life table which compares Kawanehonchō to all other cities and towns in Shizuoka Prefecture. On the average, men in Kawanehonchō on their 65th birthday had almost 20 years (19.92 years) of healthy life expectancy, and over 25 years (25.71 years) for women in 2017 (Shizuoka Prefecture Homepage 2017). Both are above the average in Shizuoka Prefecture, and Shizuoka Prefecture ranks the second longest healthy life expectancy among all the prefectures in Japan in 2016 (Shizuoka Prefecture Homepage 2020). Over the past decade, the town was featured in various magazines and TV programs for its healthy life expectancy.

Getting Further Insights on Kawanehonchō Based on Recent Censuses

To find which age cohorts of senior citizens were affected by migration and by how much, we used the census-survival rate (forward) method on Kawanehonchō census data for 2005 and 2010 to project the age-specific number of survivors to expect in 2015 (Table 2.1). The projection method assumes that the rate of census net undercount remains the same for each particular age cohort from one census to the next and that the age-specific death rates remain constant. Because the size of the age cohort cannot be affected by future births into it, then the difference between the actual and expected number of survivors is attributable to net inmigration or net outmigration. (For a technical discussion of the projection method, the interested reader should consult Shyrock and Siegel 1976.)

Table 2.1 Net Migration of People Aged 60 or Older to
Kawanehonchō in 2010–15

Age in 2005	Pop. # 2005*	Pop. # 2010*	Forward Census Sur. Rate	Pop. # 2015*	Pop. Estimate 2015	Net Migration 2010–15
55–59	699	575				
60–64	629	686	0.9814	578	564	14
65–69	783	603	.9587	668	658	10
70–74	899	736	.9400	566	567	−1
75–79	840	794	.8832	653	650	3
80–84	551	690	.8214	661	652	9
85–89	295	380	.6897	488	476	12
90–94	104	166	.5627	228	214	14
95–99	38	34	0.2568**	53	52	5
100+	6	4		4		
Total	4,844	4,668		3,899	3,833	66

* These counts are from the censuses of Kawanehonchō in the years stated.

** The survival rate from ages 90 or older to ages 95 or older = 38÷148 = 0.2568. Multiply that quotient by the total count of people counted at ages 90 or older in 2010 (= 204) to find the estimate of 52 survivors to the 2015 population count. Because there were actually 57 people counted in the census in 2015 at ages 95 or older, we estimate that there was a net inmigration of 5, but it likely represented a retention of people who might otherwise have moved.

Table 2.1 shows that the two five-year age cohorts of elderly people with the largest net inmigration to Kawanehonchō in 2010–2015 were aged 60–64 and 90–94 in 2015. For example, the population aged 55–59 in 2005 (699) who survived to ages 60–64 in 2010 numbered 686 in 2010. The forward census survival rate was 0.9814 (= 686÷699). In 2010, there were 575 people aged 55–59 who were eligible to survive to be 60–64 in the 2015 census. Their survival rate was assumed to remain the same for people aged 55–59 in the previous 5-year interval (0.9814). Thus, the expected number of people in

Kawanehonchō aged 60–64 in 2015 was 564 (=0.9814 X 575). However the census count was 578. Thus, it is estimated that the 60–64 age cohort had a net inmigration of 14 people to Kawanehonchō. It is reasonable to think that the 60–64-year-olds were new retirees. The other five-year age cohort show- ing a net inmigration of 14 people was aged 90–94 in 2015. Possibly they were returning to Kawanehonchō in conjunction with the net inmigration of 14 people aged 60–64, who could have been their newly retired children. Or maybe the success of the eldercare programs retained more people aged 85– 89 in 2010 who would have otherwise moved away. A third interpretation is that, contrary to our assumption that age-specific death rates remained con- stant, the rates may have fallen in response to the success of the elder care programs. Future research is needed to clarify which one(s) of these interpre- tations are plausible. We shall address the issues of migration in Kawanehonchō further in Chapter 9.

Structural Support for Healthy Aging

The Kawanehonchō municipal government divided the elderly into two main groups, "requiring support levels 1 and 2" and "requiring care levels 1 to 5" (see Chapter 1 for further explanation of these levels in the LTCI system). To prevent the elderly from entering the first level, or prevent them from level- ing up in the LTCI system, various public and private services are provided to the elderly. Kaneko (2009) explains that rural areas tend to have more elderly who engage in agriculture and forestry that limit their time and activities, and these elders would lack the time to participate in social, leisure, and cultural activities until they retire. Even if they hope to find activities to fulfill their purpose of life after retirement, it is more difficult for them to seek such ac- tivities on their own. In addition, in urban areas, there are various options for private-sector organizations for the elderly. Thus, in depopulating towns, the role of the public and private organizations is extremely important in under- standing the needs of the elderly and the ways of providing services to them and to their caregivers (Kaneko 2009). As mentioned earlier, Kawanehonchō is known for having long disability-free years of life. Thus, a key to under- standing healthy aging appears to lie in these services.

Currently, at Kawanehonchō, there are mainly two offices that organize and provide services for the elderly who do not need immediate LTCI—the Kawanehonchō municipal welfare office and the Kawanehonchō Council of Social Welfare (KCSW). The major difference is that the KCSW is a non-profit, private-sector organization while the municipal social welfare office is public. At Kawanehonchō, some of the employees at the municipal government office were transferred to the KCSW when it was established in 2005, the year that Kawanehonchō was established by merging two neighboring towns. Local people call the municipal welfare office "*yakuba*," meaning town hall, and the KCSW "*shakyō*" (Japanese official name of Council of Social Welfare, *Shakai Fukushi Kyōgikai,* for short). The close ties of these offices providing support for the elderly may have caused difficulty in drawing the line in figuring tasks between the two offices, but it allows their collaborations and more choices in programs and activities in which the elderly can participate.

Overview of Kawanehonchō Municipal Welfare Office (Yakuba)

The Kawanehonchō municipal welfare office offers various disability-preventive programs for the elderly. One of its goals is to promote the integrated community care system (*chiiki hōkatsu care system*), defined as "a mechanism by which various forms of support are provided in a continuous and comprehensive manner in accordance with the situation of each elderly person and changes in that situation, with the long-term care insurance services as the core" (Morikawa 2014, 4). Community general support centers were mandated to implement initiatives, such as promoting preventive self-care for seniors, comprehensive long-term care consultation, and support for continuous care management (Morikawa 2014). Although the system is a government-created scheme as discussed in Chapter 1, in regards to how to deliver such preventive services, great emphasis was placed on the autonomy of each municipality in identifying and utilizing local resources. For a small rural town like Kawanehonchō, the support center is located and managed by the Kawanehonchō municipal welfare office.

As part of promoting the integrated community care system, municipal welfare office employees (hereinafter referred to as "municipal employees") visit 30 community centers covering various geographical districts of Kawanehonchō to teach exercises to prevent disability and dementia. During the two-to-three-hour program for the elderly, they also offer basic health check-ups and teach elderly people about such relevant social issues as changes in care systems and crimes targeted on the elderly. Municipal employees plan and offer these programs about three times a month at each center in rotation. They also arrange transportation for the elderly who cannot travel by foot. The numbers of people participating in these programs vary by region, some regions having close to 20 participants; and some having more than 50 participants. Employees from the municipal welfare office take turns, and usually about two or three of them lead the program at the community center supported by local volunteers of each district and staff from non-profit organizations.

The municipal welfare office offers programs for caregivers as well. The "Carer's Café" (caretaker's café) aims to provide respite care through ideas and support for the care providers. Municipal employees offer such meetings about 12 times a year at various locations; they make suggestions to those who provide care for the elderly at home and listen to their concerns and health issues. It is an important resource for caregivers in Kawanehonchō, since they are aging as well. One of the cafés offers a hot spring bathing facility and a dining room where the caregivers can eat lunch with their friends. Municipal employees also offer basic health check-ups and occasionally bring experts to teach exercises that postpone disability among the caregivers. Some elderly are also caregivers, so they participate in programs for both elderly and caregivers.

Besides the municipal Kawanehonchō welfare office, the Lifelong Learning division of the Kawanehonchō municipal government offers about five annual classes about gardening, exercising, and singing that targets women 60 years old and older.[1] They also offer about five enrichment classes for the elderly men and women over 70 years old.[2]

Overview of the Kawanehonchō Council of
Social Welfare (Shakyō)

Depopulating towns like Kawanehonchō lack wide ranges of private social welfare corporations. Thus, the role of the Kawanehonchō Council of Social Welfare (KCSW) is especially important in promoting healthy aging. Employees of the KCSW support and organize volunteers and provide services for people with disabilities. They also provide daycare services for the elderly on the first floor of the KCSW office. The KCSW further organizes programs to support health and independence for the elderly through an emphasis on preventive care. There are three other locations of day service centers where the elderly can chat, paint, exercise, and sing with their friends. For those who lack access to the day service centers, transportation is provided. At least two employees who are also certified as care workers support these elderly by providing exercises and suggestions for their lifestyles at these centers. Various artistic activities require cognitive skills and manual dexterity. Examples of these activities include calligraphy, origami, and art made from caps from plastic bottles. The elderly participants usually work in groups of about five elderly, and many participants are women. While they engage in arts and crafts as a group, the participants create a sense of community through their conversations.

One of the centers in the Okuizumi district (Ikoi no ie) is located at a former kindergarten facility that closed due to the declining birth rate. The smaller building with a triangular roof in Figure 2.8 is the former kindergarten facility and also the center where the elderly gather. The larger white building on the right is a former elementary school that is no longer in use due to the declining birth rate. The elementary school building cannot be used for other civic purposes until it can be remodeled to meet new, strict building codes to prevent structural damage from earthquakes. At the center in the former kindergarten facility, elderly people can spend the whole day for US $3, and eat lunch for US $2. Many elderly people visit such centers two or three days per week.

As mentioned earlier, since Kawanehonchō covers a geographically wide area, there are 30 community centers covering all the geographical districts, each community organizing a meeting called a "salon" at their local commu-

Figure 2.8 Ikoi no ie at Okuizumi District of Kawanehonchō

Photo provided by Kimiko Tanaka

nity centers. The elderly in each of the salons gather and decide meeting schedules and goals for each month and throughout the year. The programs the municipal welfare office offers are considered events to take place at each salon. Staff members from the KCSW contact the municipal welfare office, the local elderly, and the volunteers, who are in charge of organizing the local salons; these stake holders decide the schedule. In addition, the staff members of KCSW support the local elderly and volunteers in planning their yearly schedule and allocate the budget of the town to each salon. They also provide transportation services when the elderly decide to travel together for salon events. Great support of the KCSW allows autonomy for the elderly in each salon in deciding their annual schedule. In fact, some districts create a booklet for the elderly in their salon to publicize the budget and the activity schedule. One of the largest salons is called Konagai Salon Hustle, which is a salon organized by people living in the Konagai district of Kawanehonchō. It is one of the most active and autonomous salons, featured by the media for its numerous civic activities: e.g., dancing, singing, exercising, and cheering local junior high school athletes at sports events.

Furthermore, there are nine senior clubs called Ikiiki Clubs at various districts offering activities such as ground golf, chorus, dance, gardening, calligraphy, and knitting. 178 men and 285 women participated in the clubs in 2020. Some districts are small, so these districts do club activities through their salons. Big districts, such as the Tokuyama region, can offer club activities (e.g., chorus, flower arrangement, and quoits) separately from the salon activities. At each club, the elders meet about once a month, and they decide the activities and the yearly schedule. Staff from KCSW look over their plans and provide funds (around US $500 to US $600 a year) from the town budget.

Grassroots Programs Supporting the Elderly

Finally, Shizuoka Prefecture initiated the idea of a welfare service that aims to surmount the barriers separating people by age and disability.[3] One of the programs to put these ideas into effect is called *ibasho*, translated as "the place we belong." How to create such an *ibasho* with local citizens is a challenge not only for Kawanehonchō but also for other towns in Shizuoka Prefecture. Some districts, such as the Umetaka district, initiate events on their own for local people, such as karaoke parties and sporting events at the community center, and they can get support from the municipal welfare office and the KCSW. There is one non-profit organization called Kawane Life. One of its programs is to create events for local mothers with young children to get together, and one of their activities is to cook and provide lunch boxes to the elderly. It also supports events offered by the municipal welfare office and the KCSW through providing volunteers.

Summary

In this chapter, we have briefly described the short sociodemographic history of Kawanehonchō. In discussing population changes, we raised the possibility of inmigration of the elderly to this town based on the census data. We also described the overview of major public and private organizations providing programs to support the elderly to remain healthy and socially in-tegrated in this town. It appears that the role of these formal organizations has increased and become a crucial factor in sustaining the collective envi-ronment linked to active life expectancy in a depopulated aging town. To observe and explain how the environment can contribute to the well-being of the elderly, we will review two concepts, collective efficacy and social capital, in the next chapter.

~ Three ~

Social Capital, Collective Efficacy, and Elderly Vitality

Émile Durkheim, one of the first sociologists, initiated the theoretical and empirical study of social integration and its impact on people's lives (L. Berkman et al. 2000; Pillemer and Glasgow 2000). Durhkeim introduced the concept of social solidarity in order to explain how individual pathology is a function of social dynamics (L. Berkman et al. 2000). He tied modern urban life to increasing alienation and the breakdown of social cohesion (Kushner and Sterk 2005). In his view, social integration was a way to cope with modernizing forces. Since then, there arose various theoretical perspectives in explaining the effects of community on the well-being of the community and the individual.

Yen and her colleagues (2009, 457) claim that research on a neighborhood's influence on older adults is quite limited, and the majority of these studies focus on the West. Their systematic review of 33 studies focusing on the neighborhood's effect on the health of older adults found that a neighborhood is described by the composition of its residents based on such census data as the median income and the percentage of those unemployed. They pointed out that the neighborhood-level socioeconomic status, the most commonly used measurement for the neighborhood characteristics in the literature, was the strongest and most consistent predictor of health outcomes. In other words, very few studies directly measured neighborhood features or context that can be related in explaining the influence of the neighborhood on health (Yen, Michael, and Perdue 2009, 460).

Collective Efficacy and Social Capital

Durkheim considered morality as a main object of his sociological study and he claimed that solidarity and regulations, or rules are two distinctive features of morality (Gofman 2019; Durkheim, Lukes, and Halls 1982; Durkheim 1984). Durkheim linked the transformation in the nature of solidarity (mechanical to organic) to how deviance is controlled. Under the conditions of mechanical solidarity, there is a high degree of control over the individuals. As communities grow in complexity, size, and density, the dominant basis of integration evolves from mechanical to organic solidarity. As societies transform from rural, mechanical solidarity to urban, organic solidarity, the collective conscience diminishes while the occupational diversity increases the complexity of social classes, and that diversifies individuals' interpretations of what is fair to them (Durkheim 1984; Webb 1972). Durkheim's theory of social solidarity has informed studies by Criminologists on how neighborhoods make a difference in crime rates. Today, we should go on to examine how social solidarity, collective efficacy, and social capital affect health and well-being (Matsaganis and Wilkin 2015; Cohen et al. 2006). To advance that goal, we shall apply the concept of social solidarity to older adults in a rural community in Japan.

Collective Efficacy

Collective efficacy is rooted in the field of Criminology as an extension of social disorganization theory, which links neighborhood characteristics to crime and disorder (Ansari 2013; Sampson, Raudenbush, and Earls 1997; Matsaganis and Wilkin 2015). The concept of collective efficacy sprang from the idea of social capital to rethink the ways that local connections among neighbors enable them to recognize problems and collectively solve them (Drakulich 2014; Cohen et al. 2006). Collective efficacy, defined as "the ability of the community to come together for the common good" (Cagney et al. 2009, 416), has been shown positively to influence individual health outcomes (Cagney et al. 2009; Thompson and Krause 1998; Cannuscio, Block, and Kawachi 2003; Galinsky, Cagney, and Browning 2012; Matsaganis and Wilkin 2015; Skrabski 2003; Cohen et al. 2006; Yen, Michael, and Perdue 2009). Collective efficacy theory underlines neighborhood social resources in the form of mutual trust and support (social cohesion) and expectations and willingness to act for the well-being of the community (informal social control) (Cagney et al. 2009, 416). The former covers the structural aspect embedded in networks of people, while the latter covers the cognitive aspect embedded in reciprocity and collective actions (Ansari 2013, 82). Willingness to intervene for the community (informal social control) assumes the existence of some network that members can trust and use to support one another (social cohesion). Both elements are necessary to reduce crime and disorder in the community. Beyond the field of Criminology, recent studies emphasized the importance of collective efficacy in avoiding premature mortality, cardiovascular disease mortality, obesity, and depression (Cohen et al. 2006; Cohen, Farley, and Mason 2003; Ahern and Galea 2011).

Availability, accessibility, and quality of collective efficacy in neighborhoods allow the elderly to remain active. Studies have shown the importance of collective efficacy on well-being, especially for the elderly as they experience frailty and decreased mobility that make them need more assistance from community members (Galinsky, Cagney, and Browning 2012; Quatrin et al. 2014; Cramm, Van Dijk, and Nieboer 2013; Matsaganis and Wilkin 2015). Using the random-digit-dialing telephone survey data of 833 residents of South Los Angeles communities, Matsaganis and Wilkin (2015) defined communicative social capital as "an information and problem-solving resource that accrues to residents as they become more integrated into their local communication network of neighbors, community organizations, and local media" (377). Communicative social capital builds collective efficacy and results in better access to health-enhancing resources. Those with better connections to communication resources within their community were more likely to feel that they can rely on their neighbors to address common problems (Matsaganis and Wilkin 2015, 383). Studies found that low health literacy is associated with patients who are older with limited education, lower income, and chronic conditions (Hickey et al. 2018). Another study pointed out that low health literacy was associated with more hospitalizations, greater use of emergency care, poorer ability to take medications appropriately, and higher mortality rates (N. Berkman et al. 2011). Thus, collective efficacy plays a crucial role in building up one's health literacy, especially those who are older with low socioeconomic status.

Pointing out that the effect of collective efficacy on depressive symptoms had not been tested in Latin America, Quatrin et al. (2014) interviewed 1,007

Brazilian elderly individuals. They found that the elderly who reported low collective efficacy had twice as high a risk of depressive symptoms as those who reported high collective efficacy, after controlling for demographic, socioeconomic, behavioral and health-related variables. They used measures developed by Sampson et al. (1997) that evaluated the degree of social cohesion and informal social control. Social cohesion was measured by questions asking how much respondents agreed that people are willing to help their neighbors, consider their neighbors as a close-knit neighborhood, trust their neighbors, whether neighbors generally get along, and whether neighbors share the same values (Sampson, Raudenbush, and Earls 1997). The informal social control was measured by residents' perceptions regarding help received from neighbors in case of such troubles occurring in the neighborhood as skipping school, wandering in the street, drawing graffiti on public buildings, showing disrespect towards adults, and assisting neighbors in critical situations. Based on the middle-aged population in the 150 sub-regions of Hungary, Skrabski, Kopp, and Kawachi (2004) interviewed 12,643 middle-aged people in 2002 and found that collective efficacy, measured by survey items in the Project on Human Development in Chicago Neighborhoods, was a significant predictor of mortality rates for both men and women after the effects of respondents' education were held constant.

Social Capital

Various scholars have used the construct of social capital to study economic development, educational attainment, the effectiveness of government, crime prevention, and the health of individuals (Snelgrove, Pikhart, and Stafford 2009; Matsaganis and Wilkin 2015; Cannuscio, Block, and Kawachi 2003; Kawachi, Kennedy, and Glass 1999). Cannuscio and colleagues (2003) defined social capital as a "public good that is provided by a group or community, and, consequently, the benefits of social capital tend to be more widely shared by members of the community" (395). Cannuscio and colleagues go on to claim that neighborhoods are a distinctive source of social capital crucial for successful aging. It has been discussed that social capital can influence the health behaviors of residents in the community in three possible pathways: (1) rapid diffusion of health information; (2) increased likelihood of adopting healthy norms and behaviors; and (3) social control over deviant health-related behaviors (Mohnen, Schneider, and Droomers

2019; Kawachi, Kennedy, and Glass 1999). Previous studies also addressed the effects of different dimensions of social capital on health.

Structural Dimension vs. Cognitive Dimension

Scholars have discussed structural and cognitive dimensions of social capital. The structural dimension focuses on externally observable aspects of social organization such as social networks and associations characterized by network connections or civic engagement. The cognitive dimension refers to subjective attitudes including trust and norms of reciprocity (Murayama et al. 2012; Baum and Ziersch 2003; Engström et al. 2008; Li et al. 2017; Hamano et al. 2010). Some studies analyze the dimensions separately, while others combine both dimensions. In Japan, some researchers found both structural social capital and cognitive social capital have significant effects on health, while others found only a positive effect of cognitive social capital on health (Murayama et al. 2012; Hibino et al. 2012; Hamano et al. 2010).

Vertical vs. Horizontal Dimension

Scholars also discussed horizontal and vertical dimensions of social capital. Horizontal social capital refers to egalitarian relationships between individuals or groups, and vertical social capital refers to the hierarchical relationships where individuals or groups interact with explicit power and authority in the society (Engström et al. 2008; Flora, Flora, and Gasteyer 2018; Murayama et al. 2012). Flora, Flora, and Gasteyer (2018) emphasize that: "horizontal social capital implies egalitarian forms of reciprocity without necessarily implying equal wealth, education, or talents... Norms of reciprocity are reinforced, but payback to the donor is not required or even expected (169–170)." Each member of the community is expected to give and receive, earning status and pleasure from contributing to the community (Flora, Flora, and Gasteyer 2018). A cross-sectional study conducted in Japan revealed that, compared to the elderly living in the highest horizontal social capital areas, the elderly living in lowest ones had a 1.25 times higher odds for having 19 or less teeth. On the other hand, vertical social capital did not show the significant association, suggesting the beneficial effects of horizontal social capital, not vertical social capital, on older Japanese adults' dental health (Aida et al. 2009).

Bonding vs. Bridging Dimension

Social capital has been divided into bonding social capital that connects individuals with similar backgrounds (homogeneous ties) and bridging social capital that connects diverse groups outside of the community (heterogeneous minds) (Flora, Flora, and Gasteyer 2018; Meijer and Syssner 2017). The dichotomy is similar to Ferdinand Tönnies's distinction between *Gemeinschaft* versus *Gesellschaft* solidarity and Durkheim's distinction between organic versus mechanical solidarity (Flora et al. 2018). When both bridging and bonding social capital are high, reinforcing each other, Flora et al. (2018) claim that it results in communities poised for action, called "entrepreneurial social infrastructure" (ESI). They discussed Aurora, Nebraska, as an example of a community with high bridging social capital attracting outsiders with affordable housing, a place for informal gathering, the community center, an excellent library, and a science museum. The community makes a significant effort to recruit newcomers into community leadership while maintaining the sense of identity (Flora and Flora 2012).

Uneven Distribution of Social Capital

Some argue that not all social capital leads to positive outcomes as social capital can restrict one's opportunities and result in more or unevenly distributed obligations by social strata (Moore et al. 2009; Rojas and Carlson 2006; Portes 2009). As Pierre Bourdieu emphasized, social capital also depends on other types of capital, including economic capital, possessed by the individuals (Bourdieu 1986). Rojas and Carson (2005, 2737) found that social capital was stratified by education and that membership in organizations was unequally distributed among educational groups.

A study based on the Cornell Retirement Migration Survey also found that education was a major factor that had a strong positive effect on the social participation among both retirement migrants and non-migrants (Brown and Glasgow 2008). Brown and Glasgow (2008) pointed out that better educated older people are more likely to develop bridging social capital while in school. It resulted in greater social networks that gave them access to greater opportunities and the ability to pay fees, dues, and transportation costs for participating in activities. They argue that more highly educated people will be healthier because they are more likely to participate in organizations, and their participation supports their health outcomes (Brown and Glasgow

2008). In other words, the effect of social capital should vary by one's socio-economic status in the United States.

Verhaeghe and Tampubolon (2012) looked at the association of individual social capital and self-rated health among the adult population in England, and they found that having friends and relatives from the intermediate class were strongly and positively associated with self-rated health. On the other hand, resources of friends and families from the manual working class was moderately and negatively related to self-rated health (Verhaeghe and Tampubolon 2012). Based on the Health and Lifestyle Survey of England, Mohan et al. (2005) found that the impact of individual social class remained statistically significant on health outcomes across all of their models, while they found little support for the association between area measures of contextual social capital and health. These results suggest that one's material circumstances mediates the relationship between contextual social capital and health (Mohan et al. 2005, 1278).

Others found the positive contextual effect of social capital beyond the social capital at the individual level (Engström et al. 2008; Kawachi, Kennedy, and Glass 1999; Poortinga 2006; Mansyur et al. 2008). Cramm et al. (2013) used the cross-sectional study of independently living older adults in Rotterdam, the Netherlands. Their multilevel analyses found that both individual social capital and neighborhood services, neighborhood social capital, and neighborhood cohesion had positive effects on the well-being of the older adults (Cramm, Van Dijk, and Nieboer 2013). Based on the cross-sectional baseline study of the Stockholm Public Health Cohort, Engström et al. (2008) found a relationship between lack of contextual social capital and poor self-rated health, after adjusting for individual level social capital and sociodemographic variables. Kawachi et al. (1999) found that after adjusting for a full range of individual level variables, residing in a state with the lowest levels of social capital (measured by the extent of civic trust, collective perception of reciprocity, and per capita membership in voluntary associations in each state) was associated with 45 percent to 73 percent increased odds of fair or poor health compared with living in the highest social-capital states. Aida et al. (2011) used trust (cognitive social capital) and volunteer participation (structural social capital) at the individual level and the community levels to investigate whether social capital changes the relationship between income inequality and health in Aichi Prefecture of Japan. They found that community-level structural social capital reduced the association between income inequality and poor self-rated health (Aida et al. 2011). In conclusion, studies in England, the Netherlands, and Japan suggest the contextual social capital to be a significant factor on health beyond the individual level social capital, or a mediating factor between health and individual level social capital.

The Need for Qualitative Study beyond the West

Both social capital and collective efficacy are important concepts for understanding the well-being of the elderly at the individual level and the contextual level. However, there are no consistent measurements for collective efficacy and multiple dimensions of social capital, and the results of these studies are inconsistent. There are certain ambiguities in existing scales of collective efficacy and social capital (Galinsky, Cagney, and Browning 2012; Whitley 2008). Since quantitative studies have a limitation in grasping how it influences health, qualitative research is suited to contribute to the resolution of methodological and conceptual ambiguities. However, very few peer-reviewed papers have been published through a qualitative lens (Whitley 2008, 99).

Today, the literature is sparse on the reasons why some communities possess a stronger sense of social capital linked to better health status (Hanibuchi et al. 2012, 226). Several scholars argued the importance of adopting a humanistic perspective within medical geography. They called for qualitative research to understand how experiences of health may be shaped by living within particular geographical and social spaces (Airey 2003). The community-based longitudinal study conducted by Wolf and Bruhn on Roseto, Pennsylvania, shed a light on its unusually low rates of cardiovascular disease in the 1950s compared to surrounding communities, and illustrated the importance of more studies specifically focusing on a specific place (ibid). Hanibuchi et al. (2012) advocated the need for more studies like the Roseto story focusing on a specific place. To investigate the effects of social capital at the individual and contextual levels and to examine the role of collective efficacy in promoting the health of the elderly, researchers must be closely acquainted with a particular local community, observe the elderly embedded in that particular sociocultural context, and consider the local people supporting them and their caregivers. However, few qualitative studies have been conducted in rural locations (Whitley 2008, 99). Also, the previous studies of the elderly focused on the elderly and excluded the voices of people supporting the facilities and the programs for them. In recent years, geographical areas (physical places) are considered social spaces where individuals subjectively experience health and health care. Recent studies used qualitative methods to explain how individuals' experiences and perceptions of "place" influence their health. Qualitative studies are valuable because they provide insight on how places influence health and health-related behaviors and show causal pathways between them (Cummins et al. 2007).

Furthermore, most studies are based on Western nations, so there is still a need to examine our research questions in non-Western nations (Meng and Chen 2014; Ichida et al. 2009). Considering the profound cultural and historical differences between Japan and Western nations, it is important to understand the relationship of social capital on elderly well-being both at the individual and the contextual levels by observing and querying the elderly at a specific social and cultural site, such as Kawanehonchō. As studies increasingly recognize the importance of neighborhoods to promote successful aging, it is essential to pay attention to the narratives of the elderly, as well as to the people supporting them in the local community, to provide in-depth explanations of whether and how collective efficacy and social capital affect the well-being of the elderly directly and indirectly.

Summary

We discussed collective efficacy and social capital as closely related concepts to explain the effect of neighborhood on the well-being of the elderly. These concepts allow us to expect that services and programs for the elderly offered in Kawanehonchō play a key role in strengthening the collective efficacy and social capital. It is important to visit the actual local context to see how they strengthened collective efficacy and social capital. In the next chapter, we will explain how we gathered multiple qualitative and quantitative data to describe and assess the link between neighborhood social resources and the well-being of the elderly.

∼ Four ∼

Research Methods and Data Collection

There are various resources of support for elderly residents of Kawanehonchō. To assess the link between neighborhood resources and the well-being of the elderly, we used six sources of data:

1) Surveys conducted by the Kawanehonchō municipal welfare office and the Kawanehonchō Council of Social Welfare (KCSW);

2) Secondary data obtained from Shizuoka Prefecture in regards to the health and lives of the elderly in Kawanehonchō;

3) Observation of the activities, programs, and facilities for the elderly in July, 2015, September and October, 2016, and July, 2017;

4) Interviews with local leaders of Kawanehonchō in July, 2015, and September and October, 2016;

5) Survey conducted by the senior author from September to November, 2016, of the elderly participating in these programs;

6) Secondary data on rural migration, and interviews of people who newly moved to Kawanehonchō or its surrounding areas in July and August, 2018.

Having multiple sources allows us to assess quantitatively and qualitatively the relationship between health and aging at both the individual and the community level.

(1) Surveys Conducted by the Kawanehonchō Municipal Welfare Office and the Kawanehonchō Council of Social Welfare (KCSW)

In Chapter 1, we explained how the municipal welfare office and the KCSW support the welfare of the elderly. Both offices conducted surveys of their local citizens to understand their challenges and needs, and the summaries of these reports were obtained from these offices. These results were especially useful in providing overviews of the town and the elderly.

(2) Secondary Data Obtained from Shizuoka Prefecture

The survey was conducted by mail based on a random sampling of the elderly in all municipalities in Shizuoka Prefecture in February, 2014 (*Shizuokaken ni okeru kōreisha seikatsu jittai chōsa*) (Shizuokaken Sōgō Kenkō Center 2016). The survey asked questions about the lifestyles and the well-being of the elderly. With support from the Kawanehonchō municipal welfare office, we could obtain the data on Kawanehonchō from this survey. Since our survey and interview data exclude elderly residents who do not participate in community activities, these secondary data provided important information on that subset of the elderly in Kawanehonchō.

(3) Observation of the Activities, Facilities, and Programs

In different districts of Kawanehonchō, various programs are offered to promote the well-being of the elderly. The first author visited four programs offered in four districts (Kuwanoyama, Konagai, Okuizumi, Kaminagao) in July, 2015. A program offered at community centers in Kuwanoyama is called Genki Hatsuratsu Kyōshitsu, an active and healthy aging program led by the municipal welfare office; programs offered at Kaminagao and Okuizumi are called Ikigai Day Service (IkiDay), led by KCSW. The program offered at Konagai is called the Konagai Salon Hustle, led by local elderly and supported by the municipal welfare office and the KCSW. After the first author introduced herself, she observed and participated in these activities, talked with the leaders of these groups, and talked with several elderly people during tea time.

In July, 2015, she also observed and interviewed people supporting the elderly at four different facilities for the elderly (Akaishinosato, Group Home Matsuoka, Kawanehonchō Fukushi Center, Kawanehonchō Kōreisha Day Service Center), all of them being a day care center, and two of them also offering short-term and long-term care to the elderly. For each of them, for approximately 90 minutes, the manager showed her around to explain their facilities, let her observe and talk with several elderly at these centers, and to allow her to interview those supporting the elderly at the end.

In September, 2016, the first author revisited the Ikigai Day Service programs/centers in Kaminagao and Okuizumi to observe and to conduct the survey and interview the elderly. She also observed a program called "Carer's café" (caretakers' café) in the Sehira community center located in the Shimonagao district. Furthermore, in September, 2016, she observed a quoits tournament and participated in an exercise class called Genki-up in October, 2016. Both activities were offered at the gym right next to the Kawanehonchō municipal office. In July, 2017, she observed another Genki Hatsuratsu Kyōshitsu in the Senzu district led by the municipal welfare office. These qualitative sources were quite useful in understanding the aging citizens in their community through the eyes the elderly and those who support the elderly in the community.

(4) Interviews with Local Leaders

In July, 2015, and September and October, 2016, the first author interviewed those who support the healthy aging of Kawanehonchō: the mayor, the staff and care managers[1] of the KCSW, the director of the integrated community care system (*chiiki hōkatsu care system*), the leaders of regional salons, an organizer of the regional senior club, and employees of elder daycare and long-term care facilities. She interviewed these people in an open-ended format lasting 15 to 40 minutes. She asked them to describe anything about their experience of aging in the town to gain their own perspectives of how to lead successful aging and their experiences in this geographic, economic, and cultural context.

(5) *Survey of the Elderly Participating in the Programs*

Previous studies lacked depth and focus on the health of the elderly participants in the community programs in Japan. To develop a culturally sensitive questionnaire, the following four Japanese surveys were used as references.

Kagawa Prefecture conducted the survey (*Kōreisha ibasho jittai chōsa*) of their elderly to understand *ibasho,* meaning "the place we belong." The survey reflects their concern over the increasing numbers of elderly people living alone. It is reported that some elderly people go to supermarkets, game centers, and coffee shops to seek an *ibasho* (Kagawa Prefectural Government 2012). The Japanese government also conducted a face-to-face survey of the elderly to ask about their social participations and relationships with their neighbors (*Kōreisha-no chiikishakai-e-no sanka-ni kansuru ishiki chōsa*) (Cabinet Office Japan 2013). Since these surveys targeted the elderly, the formatting and the language used in the surveys were helpful in designing our questionnaire to assess their social participation and neighborhood relations that are appropriate for the elderly.

Another survey that the Japanese government conducted assessed people's perceptions of lowered fertility rates, the family, and the local community (*Shōshika taisaku to kazoku, chiiki no kizuna-ni kansuru isiki chōsa*) (Cabinet Office Japan 2006). Finally a survey conducted by the city of Yokohama (Kōnan Ward) assessed their residents' perception of their neighbors (*Kōnan kumin ishiki chōsa*) (City of Yokohama 2013). These surveys were targeted on all the adults, but they included questions assessing the quality of the neighborhood community based on experience in interacting with neighbors and thoughts about neighborhood relations. These surveys were helpful in understanding what kind of things are considered important in building relationships with neighbors.

Based on these sources, we developed a questionnaire to ask questions of the elderly participants about the social activities in which they participate, their neighbors (how they think about neighborhood relations, degree of neighborhood relations, what they consider important in thinking of relationships with neighbors), the kinds of support they provide or receive from their neighbors, and what they consider important in building relationships with their neighbors. The answers allowed us to judge the depth and the quality of neighborhood interactions as measurements of contextual social capital and collective efficacy. We also included the questions to assess participants' activities of daily living (ADLs), self-rated health, as well as their age, marital status, housing, number of children, co-residence, and standard of living. We also included open ended questions at the end of the survey to ask the elderly about *ikigai*, the purpose of life, and the kind of town Kawanehonchō is for the elderly. After the survey questionnaire was made, the first author consulted with municipal employees to confirm that the questions were appropriate in terms of length and language. To make it easier for the elderly to respond, we shortened the survey questionnaire from the original.

These resources guided our understanding of the elderly's everyday lives and behaviors to determine the role of the community on health and illness. From September to November, 2016, the first author visited programs for the elderly offered by the KCSW and the Kawanehonchō municipal office. Fifty-eight survey questionnaires were completed owing to the great support from these offices in arranging dates, times, and places for the elderly to distribute the surveys.

(6) Interviews of People Newly Migrated to Surrounding Areas

Census data showed the possibility of retirement migration towards Kawanehonchō (See Table 2.1 in Chapter 2). However, finding such people was extremely difficult. Contacting people at the municipal government and the non-profit organizations, we conclude that there are not many older adults migrating to Kawnehonchō after retirement. Some suspect that these migrants are those who came back to the town possibly after the retirement to take care of their elderly parents. As these people do not tend to participate in programs with their elderly parents, it was difficult to find these people by observing programs. With the help of local people, the first author visited the community of newcomers living right outside of Kawanehonchō in July and August, 2018, and interviewed them about the reasons they moved. We also included the descriptive statistics from the survey conducted by the Mitsubishi Research Institute in 2013 based on those who hope to move to rural areas. It gave us a bigger picture on rural migration.

Summary

These multiple sources of quantitative and qualitative data allowed us to analyze the link between community networks and the well-being of the elderly from different angles to see the issue more fully. In the next chapter, results from the surveys conducted by the Kawanehonchō municipal welfare office, the KCSW, and from the secondary data obtained from Shizuoka Prefecture will be discussed. Observations of activities of the elderly are described in Chapter 6, and interviews with leaders are summarized in Chapter 7. Results from our own survey of the elderly participating in these activities are presented in Chapter 8. Interviews of retired migrants to the surrounding areas of Kawanehonchō are discussed in Chapter 9. Our usage of personal interviews of a convenience sample of the inmigrants shed light in rural inmigration in Japan. Finally, we synthesize our findings from these diverse sources in Chapter 10 and explore the implications for future research.

～ Five ～

Identifying Strengths and Challenges through Existing Surveys

To identify what the elderly need to achieve healthy aging, surveys were conducted at the prefectural level and municipal level. The Kawanehonchō Council of Social Welfare (KCSW) conducted a survey of local citizens and junior and high school students. Also, KCSW carried out focus groups of workers at the facilities for the elderly in order to assess and revise their programs. The Kawanehonchō municipal office also surveyed the elderly to give them a voice in the planning of welfare programs to serve them. Finally, Shizuoka Prefecture conducted a survey of all the towns and villages in the prefecture. These publicly available resources are useful in grasping issues surrounding the elderly in Kawanehonchō.

Identifying the Needs through the Survey and Focus Groups by KCSW

KCSW conducted a mail survey from June to July, 2014, of local citizens. The reason was to set up goals to build the town in a way that provides safety for everyone. A survey research center mailed 1,000 surveys to local adults over 20 years old, who were randomly sampled based on the registry of residential addresses. The total number of respondents was 470 (Kawanehonchō Council of Social Welfare 2015). Also, 105 junior and high school students received questionnaires and 104 students responded. Furthermore, they conducted focus groups on groups who support the elderly and salon members.

Nearly 90 percent of the adult respondents knew about KCSW. Overall, many recognized the importance of sustaining the neighborhood networks to continue local community activities and evacuation drills in case of natural disasters. More than 80 percent of adult respondents reported that they could support one another in the community in case of natural disasters; over 60 percent, that they have family members or neighbors who could help them in case of an emergency. In case of needing support, nearly 70 percent believe that their residents do support one another. Especially the elderly found neighborhood relations to be extremely important; it reflects the increasing number of the elderly people living alone and/or taking care of their parents and their spouses by themselves. On the other hand, working-age people do not see the necessity of neighborhood networks as much as the elderly. It is becoming a challenge to maintain close neighborhood networks that involve people from all generations (Kawanehonchō Council of Social Welfare 2015).

Nearly 50 percent of the adult respondents have participated in volunteering activities; over 65 percent started as part of their local community activities. There is a trend of older unemployed generations hoping to participate in volunteering activities. On the other hand, about 46 percent of adult respondents had never participated in volunteer activities due to a lack of time and easily available opportunities as well as health related reasons (Kawanehonchō Council of Social Welfare 2015). When it comes to junior high and high school students, over 60 percent had never participated in the volunteering activities, although 60 percent considered that learning about social welfare would give them useful experiences to draw upon in their future work and family lives.

Based on the focus groups, the KCSW also recognized that the people who participated as volunteers tend to be older and women. The program would be impossible without volunteers. However, the homogeneity of the volunteers could intimidate new volunteers. Reflecting these voices, the KCSW concluded that it is important to diversify volunteer opportunities and members, especially student volunteers (Kawanehonchō Council of Social Welfare 2015).

Furthermore, the focus groups pointed out the differences in the scale and the activeness among salons. It reflected the population density of the districts. Some salons have more volunteers, leaders, and participants. But for small salons, the same people end up leading them and some activities become routinized or deactivated. As people leading salons get older, especially in districts with extremely low population density, their needs and the roles of KCSW in assisting them become crucial for the survival of salons. Having the same elderly leading salons can also prevent their children from participating as volunteers.

Learning from Surveys — Kawanehonchō Municipal Office

In January, 2014, the Kawanehonchō municipal office conducted a mail-in survey to randomly selected 1,994 people 65 and above based on the registry of residential address. The response rate was high, 80.6 percent (N = 1,607). They also mailed the survey to 456 people who were certified of needed long-term care at home (requiring care or support levels discussed in Chapter 2) and 292 people (64.0 percent) responded.

Based on the survey mailed to the randomly sampled elderly 65 and above, nearly 40 percent responded their health was well, close to 40 percent responded normal, and about 20 percent of the elderly responded not well. To keep themselves healthy, more than half of the elderly responded to rest and sleep well; about 46 percent responded that they are careful with what they eat; 36 percent try their best to look after themselves; about 27 percent found walking and participating in sports to be helpful; about 25 percent find it important to think positively; and about 22 percent found working and health check-ups to be important.

More than natural disasters (16.7 percent) and financial matters (11.6 percent), what they are concerned about the most is their health (59.6 percent) and the well-being of their family members (44.4 percent). Only 5.4 percent of the elderly were concerned about social isolation and less than 5 percent were concerned about the relationship with family members and friends (Kawanehonchō 2015). When they require someone to provide physical care, the majority of them hope for aging in place. About 26 percent of the elderly responded that they hope to stay home and be taken care of only by family members, while a great proportion of the elderly (36.5 percent) hope to stay home while utilizing home-care and day care services, about 15 percent hope to enter the nursing homes, and about 16 percent do not have any plans. When it comes to the time for their family members to require some physical care, about 22 percent hope to take care of them at home by family members, and again the most popular response was to stay home while getting some support including daycare centers and home-care services (42.1 percent). Only 10.4 percent hope to rely on nursing homes and 14 percent did not have any thoughts. Reflecting such a strong wish of aging in place, more than 30 percent of the elderly hope for the improvements of services and programs that allow them to remain healthy and allow them to stay in their home (Kawanehonchō 2015).

The survey on those classified as requiring support or care levels included several questions to their caregivers. Descriptive statistics show that the major caregivers are women (66 percent). Nearly 20 percent of these caregivers are in their 50s; 33 percent, in their 60s; 23.1 percent, in their 70s; and over 17 percent, in their 80s or above. Thus, what these caregivers consider the most challenging is the emotional and physical burden (42.0 percent), which was greater than the financial burden (19.3 percent). While about 46 percent of these caregivers considered it challenging to take care of the elderly at home due to time constraints and about 36 percent found it challenging due to physical burden, about 10 percent of them responded that they want to take care of the elderly at home just by family members, and about 60 percent of them hope to take care of the elderly family members at home while getting some support from public welfare services (Kawanehonchō 2015).

Frequent Use of Surveys to Improve Organizations

Not only were these results helpful to understand the elderly, but also the availability and transparency of such data suggest the existence of horizontal social capital, the egalitarian relationship between individuals and groups in the town. Both the municipal office and the KCSW gathered information to listen to voices of the caregivers, elderly, students, and volunteers to identify the needs. Based on these results, the KCSW recognized the importance of diversifying opportunities, and supporting districts that attempt to create grassroots social groups regardless of age and disability to diversify groups, volunteers, and participants[1] (Kawanehonchō Council of Social Welfare 2015). Based on the results, the municipal office responded to the necessity of developing a better integrated care system that allows the elderly to age in place by getting support from public services. Surveys and transparency in sharing the results and the proposals make the town a very ideal model for shared governance. Responding to such needs, their programs for the elderly emphasized their availability for services including visiting their hospital if they become hospitalized to process the paper work to receive the home care support. They emphasized these services to the elderly, as the elderly tend to assume these are family responsibilities. To improve access to medical care services, KCSW offers a vehicle and the local people could ask for volunteer drivers to get to the hospital. The municipal office also offers transportation support for the cost of US $12 to US $25 for halfway to a nearby city (about 40 minutes to one hour drive) depending on the location of their house in the town. The town is also developing a virtual hospital as it lacks an advanced hospital. At four clinics in the town, the elderly can talk with the doctors in hospitals while these doctors, nurses, care managers, and family members share information of the patients to provide the best support.

Learning from the Survey Conducted by Shizuoka Prefecture

Shizuoka Prefecture conducted a survey of the elderly in February, 2014, (*Shizuokaken ni okeru kōreisha seikatsu jittai chōsa*) including Kawanehonchō (Shizuokaken Sōgō Kenkō Center 2016). They asked various questions of the elderly 65 and above, and we could obtain the data on Kawanehonchō from this survey.[2] Table 5.1 provides descriptive statistics of variables that relate to physical and mental well-being of the elderly, as well as their degree of collective efficacy and social capital. The sample size was 389 (192 men and 197 women). The age of respondents varied from 65 to 83 years old for both men and women (average 74 years old). On the average, the elderly have lived in Kawanehonchō for 60 years for men and 52 years for women. The majority of the respondents are married (85 percent for men and 63 percent for women), and about half of the elderly men and women live in a one-generational household. That only 14 percent of men and 11 percent of women live in a three-generational household suggests the difficulty of continuing three-generational households in Kawanehonchō today. The majority of the elderly completed middle-school (61 percent for men and 65 percent for women), and 27 percent completed their high school education. Less than 10 percent completed a college degree. On average, a majority of the elderly responded their standard of living to be in the middle (50 percent for men and 60 percent for women), and greater than 30 percent of male and female respondents answered that they were lower middle or low.

Table 5.1 Descriptive Statistics from 2014 Survey of the Elderly in Shizuoka Prefecture.

	Men (%)	Women (%)
Health check-ups		
Once a year	157 (84)	162 (85)
Once in several years	25 (13)	21 (11)
Never	5 (3)	8 (4)
Frequency of visiting home doctors		
Never	14 (7)	19 (10)
A couple of times a year	46 (24)	53 (27)
1 to 3 times a month	125 (66)	120 (62)
1 to 2 times a week	0 (0)	1 (.5)
3 to 4 times a week	3 (2)	0
Almost everyday	1 (1)	1 (.5)
Reasons for visiting doctors		
Stroke	12 (6)	7 (4)
High blood pressure	85 (45)	103 (54)
Heart disease	19 (10)	13 (7)
Cancer	17 (9)	8 (4)
Diabetes	31 (17)	19 (10)
Dental treatment	51 (27)	30 (16)
Muscle joint	17 (9)	32 (17)
Gastrointestinal Health	14 (7)	19 (10)
Lipid abnormality	20 (11)	55 (29)
Sleeping disorder	4 (2)	12 (6)
Lung	13 (7)	2 (1)
Fracture	4 (2)	4 (2)
Mental health	3 (2)	3 (2)

Distance to the home doctor

Within 3.0 km	69 (37)	91 (50)
Within 5.0 km	30 (16)	28 (15)
Within 10.0km	28 (15)	31 (17)
Within 30.0 km	18 (10)	16 (9)
Within 50.0 km	26 (14)	9 (5)
50.0 km and above	14 (8)	7 (4)

Exercise for more than 30 minutes

Never	57 (31)	64 (33)
1 to 2 times a week	45 (25)	47 (24)
3 to 4 times a week	41 (22)	45 (23)
More than 5 times a week	40 (22)	37 (19)

Walk more than 30 minutes

Never	57 (31)	58 (30)
1 to 2 times a week	50 (27)	61 (32)
3 to 4 times a week	36 (20)	37 (19)
More than 5 times a week	41 (22)	36 (19)

Work (gardening, farming, carpentering, household chores) more than 30 minutes

Never	26 (14)	20 (10)
1 to 2 times a week	44 (24)	18 (10)
3 to 4 times a week	35 (18)	38 (20)
More than 5 times a week	82 (44)	115 (60)

Growing vegetables at home

Yes	128 (67)	148 (76)
No	63 (33)	46 (24)

Green Tea Intake

Never	6 (3)	8 (4)
1 to 3 cups a day	40 (21)	28 (14)
4 to 6 cups a day	94 (49)	101 (51)
More than 7 cups a day	51 (27)	60 (30)

Interaction with people under 20

Almost never	87 (47)	68 (35)
Less than once a week	39 (21)	56 (29)
2 to 4 times a week	35 (19)	32 (17)
More than 5 times a week	24 (13)	36 (19)

Interaction with friends

Almost never	19 (10)	16 (8)
Once a week or less	46 (25)	37 (19)
2 to 4 times a week	78 (42)	81 (42)
More than 5 time a week	44 (24)	60 (31)

Trust in friends and relatives

They are untrustworthy	2 (1)	2 (1)
They are somewhat untrustworthy	1 (1)	3 (2)
Neither	26 (14)	20 (10)
They are somewhat trustworthy	44 (23)	44 (23)
They are trustworthy	116 (61)	124 (64)

Friends and relatives being helpful to others

They only think of themselves	4 (2)	8 (4)

They tend to think of themselves first	1 (1)	1 (1)
Neither	74 (39)	54 (29)
They make some effort to help others	28 (15)	26 (14)
They always try to help others	81 (43)	100 (53)

I have more occasions of interacting with someone whose background (sex, age, standard of living) is close to mine

I agree with the statement	58 (31)	71 (39)
I somewhat agree with it	74 (39)	81 (44)
I somewhat disagree with it	29 (15)	12 (7)
I disagree with the statement	28 (15)	20 (11)

I have more occasions of interacting with someone whose background is different from mine

I agree with the statement	22 (12)	26 (14)
I somewhat agree with it	61 (32)	63 (34)
I somewhat disagree with it	51 (27)	43 (23)
I disagree with the statement	55 (29)	53 (29)

I participate in volunteer activities

Almost never	107 (58)	112 (62)
Once a week	66 (36)	58 (32)
2 to 4 times a week	12 (6)	10 (6)
More than 5 times a week	0 (0)	1 (1)

Caring for other people

Yes	12 (6)	26 (14)
No	177 (94)	164 (86)

I think positively

I disagree with the statement	2 (1)	1 (1)
I somewhat disagree with it	23 (12)	16 (8)
I somewhat agree with it	96 (51)	100 (52)
I agree with the statement	68 (36)	76 (39)

Feeling isolated

Almost never	128 (68)	119 (62)
Neither	34 (18)	29 (15)
Occasionally	20 (11)	39 (20)
Always	7 (4)	6 (3)

Days feeling not mentally well

Never	94 (50)	82 (43)
A couple of days in a month	81 (43)	87 (46)
A week in a month	8 (4)	9 (5)
Two weeks in a month or more	4 (3)	13 (7)

Self-rated health

Poor	6 (3)	5 (3)
Somewhat poor	30 (16)	26 (13)
Neither	48 (25)	38 (20)
Somewhat well	58 (31)	81 (42)
Well	47 (25)	44 (23)

Marital Status

Married	161 (85)	122 (63)
Others	28 (15)	71 (37)

Education

About up to 12 years old	10 (5)	12 (6)
About up to 15 years old	115 (61)	125 (65)
About up to 18 years old	51 (27)	51 (27)
More than 19 years old	12 (6)	5 (3)

Standard of living

Low	15 (8)	17 (9)
Lower middle	52 (27)	44 (24)
Middle	95 (50)	112 (60)
Upper middle	24 (13)	14 (7)
High	4 (2)	0 (0)

Generational co-residence

One generation	98 (56)	90 (48)
Two generations	51 (29)	75 (40)
Three generations	25 (14)	21 (11)
Four generations or more	2 (1)	2 (1)

Age	74.22 (SD=5.40)	74.48 (SD=5.20)
Years of living at Kawanehonchō	60.05 (SD=20.58)	52.24 (SD=18.20)
N	192	197

Data source: Shizuokaken Sōgō Kenkō Center

Table 5.1 also shows that most of the elderly in Kawanehonchō visit their home doctors for health check-ups at least once a year, and many of them frequently visit their home doctors despite the fact that 47 percent of the men and 35 percent of the women live further than five kilometers (3.1 miles) from their home doctor. Transportation services arranged by the Kawanehonchō municipal office and KCSW help them overcome the distance. High blood pressure is a popular reason for visiting doctors (45 percent for men and 54 percent for women); the second most common reason was dental treatment for men (27 percent) and lipid abnormality for women (29 percent). As the town is famous for green tea, most of the elderly drink more than three cups a day. Based on the data from Shizuoka Prefecture, Oguni (2000) looked at whether the areas producing green tea had a lower rate of cancer. He found that for both men and women, rates of stomach cancer and certain other cancers were significantly lower in green-tea-growing areas (Oguni 2000). The fact that only nine percent of men and four percent of women visit doctors for cancer may reflect the anti-carcinogenic properties of green tea.

Furthermore, the table suggests that the majority of people almost never felt isolated is consistent with the result of the municipal office survey discussed above. As the town lost young people due to postwar urbanization, a majority of the elderly do not have frequent interaction with younger generations. On the other hand, a majority of the elderly interact with their friends at least two to four times a week; the majority responded that they trust their friends and relatives, and 43 percent of men and 53 percent of women find that their friends and relatives are always trying to be helpful to others. Being geographically isolated from other areas, many responded that they tend to interact with someone whose background such as age, sex, and standard of living are the same; thus the majority disagreed that they have more occasions to interact with those whose backgrounds are different. These results suggest greater bonding social capital over bridging social capital.

Half of the men and 43 percent of the women never felt mentally unwell for a single day in a month, and about 43 percent of men and 46 percent of women felt mentally unwell only for a couple of days in a month. Thirty-six percent of men and 39 percent of women agreed with the statement that they think positively, and about half of both genders somewhat agree with the statement. A majority of them rated their health to be well or somewhat well.

A majority of them exercise, walk, and garden for more than 30 minutes at least once or twice a week, and a majority of them grow vegetables at home. Overall, these descriptive statistics suggest that the elderly in Kawanehonchō are mentally and physically healthy. It is possible that these positive health outcomes are linked to their neighborhood community.

To examine the association between collective efficacy and available health measures in the secondary data, partial correlations were examined. One of two elements in collective efficacy, social cohesion, was measured by their trust in most friends and relatives: 1 meaning untrustworthy and 5 meaning trustworthy (Table 5.1). Another element, informal social control, was measured by their perception of friends and relatives' willingness to help others, 1 meaning that they only thinking of themselves and 5 meaning that they always trying to be helpful to others. For health outcomes, we used available variables, self-rated health and whether respondents think positively, both measured as ordinal variables, 1 meaning respondents think negatively and rated their health poor, and 5 meaning they think positively and rated their health well (Table 5.1).

Controlling for age, sex, marital status, education, and standard of living, the partial correlation between respondents' perception of trust and self-rated health was positive ($r=.125$, $p<.05$). The partial correlation between respondents' perception of friends and relatives' willingness to help others and self-rated health was also positive ($r= .150$, $p<0.01$). The partial correlation between respondents' perception of trust and positive thinking was also positive ($r= .218$, $p<.001$); and the partial correlation between their perception of friends and relatives' willingness to help others and positive thinking was positive as well ($r= .308$, $p<.001$). Although the variables are limited, these results suggest the positive effect of social cohesion and informal social control on the health of the elderly. Previous studies discussed in Chapter 3 pointed out the effect of education on well-being. Controlling for age, sex, marital status, and the standard of living, the partial correlation between education and self-rated health was not significant ($r = .033$, $p>.05$). The same result was found for the partial correlation between education and thinking positively ($r= -.065$, $p>.05$). Contrary to previous Western studies, individual education level does not seem to significantly contribute to the well-being among the elderly living in Kawanehonchō.

Summary

These results suggest the importance of collective efficacy in promoting healthy aging beyond socioeconomic status, marital status, sex, and age. However, these secondary data did not specifically ask about the participation in services and programs that public and private organizations offer. Also, there is a lack of varieties of measurement for collective efficacy and health outcomes. Furthermore, they are limited in grasping how collective efficacy and the contextual social capital are linked to the achievement of being one of the healthiest aging towns despite not having higher educational attainment or advanced hospitals. In the next chapter, programs and activities offered at Kawanehonchō are discussed in detail through observations to add depth in understanding how collective efficacy and social capital contribute to the healthy aging of the rural town.

∽ Six ∽

Connecting the Elderly to the Neighborhood Community

We described the services from public and private organizations in Chapters 2 and 5. Also, there we discussed the crucial responses of these organizations to massive structural changes. We emphasized that the government placed great emphasis on each municipality in identifying local resources. The first author made in-depth observations of these various programs in Kawanehonchō in Summer 2015, Fall 2016, and Summer 2017. She observed Genki Hatsuratsu Kyōshitsu, an active and healthy aging program offered by the municipal welfare office. She also observed Ikigai Day Service programs/centers (IkiDay) offered by the Kawanehonchō Council of Social Welfare (KCSW). In addition, she visited the Konagai Salon Hustle, one of the largest salons in Kawanehonchō. She also observed a quoits tournament and the exercise group called Genki-up, offered at the public gymnasium located right next to the municipal welfare office. Finally, she observed a program targeted to the caregivers called "Carer's Café" (caretaker's café).

Genki Hatsuratsu Kyōshitsu at Salons

The Kawanehonchō municipal welfare office offers programs for the elderly called Genki Hatsuratsu Kyōshitsu, an active and healthy aging program, at each local salon. Since Kawanehonchō is geographically stretched out, there are about 30 local salons covering the regional districts. The first author observed this program in two separate districts in 2015 and 2017. The district of Kuwanoyama is located in a less populated area, where there were 15 elderly (three men and 12 women) participating in the program in July,

2015. There were three municipal employees leading the program and three volunteers supporting it. Another district, which is in East Senzu, is a more populated area, where there were 17 elderly residents (two men and 15 women) participating in the program in July, 2017. Clearly, the majority of participants in these programs are elderly women.

For the elderly who do not have access to local community centers, transportation can be arranged. However, although Kawanehonchō has many gently sloping uphill roads, for both districts all the elderly walked to the community center. When the first author asked a volunteer about absence, she said that almost everyone was there; most will participate even if it rains. Each district has a very good contact network in circulating the handouts about event schedules. In addition, friends in the neighborhood will remind the elderly in person by calling them or in person. Such strong networks of support built into the local community are good examples of structural social capital where it is easy for the elderly to get information on where these events take place, and they are in the layers of networks to receive reminders. These programs not only provide the elderly opportunities for the social participation, but also allow the elderly to be familiar with and establish a friendly relationship with municipal employees through face-to-face conversations, so that they know whom they need to consult when they experience any concerns about them, their families, their neighbors, and their communities.

Each program lasts about two hours. In both districts, everyone gathers at the community center by 9 A.M. The elderly participants prepare seats and clean up their community center, along with volunteer members. Collective decision making in organizing events for the salon surely gives the elderly participants a feeling of social engagement and commitment. Between 9 A.M. and 9:30 A.M., municipal employees who are also public health nurses, social workers, or care managers, greet each one of them by name and take their blood pressure. Although they cover the same topic at each salon, each elderly person and each district are different. Municipal employees do not mechanically run the same program everywhere. They have meetings before and after each salon, and they revise their program. They also review the list of people participating in the program at each salon so that they can talk with each elderly person individually, not as one participant of many. "Good morning, Misae-san. How are you? How is your grandchild?" "I am so glad to see you Michiko-san. How is your garden recently?" "Did you go to the routine health check-up, Mishima-san? I think it is almost due for the annual check-up." While municipal employees take their blood pressure, they talk with each elderly person about his or her family and friends, as a way to understand any changes possibly influencing the health of the elderly person, as well as to identify whether he or she is socially isolated. If municipal employees identify any socially isolated elderly, they stop by their houses to encourage them to participate in the programs to prevent them from further social isolation.

The actual program starts around 9:30 AM, and the program runs about one hour. The program is well-planned, well-adjusted, engaging, and enjoyable for the elderly. Mainly five municipal employees work tirelessly by constantly thinking how the elderly would view the program. Their workload and responsibility are unimaginably great in designing, developing, and administering the program, specifically designed to fit the needs of the local elderly at different locations. In designing these programs, municipal employees do not simply print out handouts they receive from the government; rather, they translate difficult terms related to policies and health into the local dialect, illustrated with pictures. Although many elderly use cell phones, most do not use the internet to seek information on the web. Thus, municipal employees create booklets or charts that are easily understood by the elderly. For exercises, they use songs and activities to make them enjoyable, and create age appropriate exercises they could try at home. They also occasionally invite a lecturer from outside the town to teach new exercises; on such an occasion, they combine people from more than three geographical districts and provide transportation services.

Topics they cover in the program include how to protect the elderly from fraud, how health care policy changes influence their lives, how to prevent dementia, how to prepare for the end of life, and how to keep healthy and active. The programs emphasize the importance for the elderly people to be informed and understand available options to be discussed with their families, medical doctors, nurses, pharmacists, volunteers, care managers, and helpers. In 2015, the major topic they covered was dementia prevention; and in 2017, the major topic was the end-of-life options.

In discussing dementia prevention, municipal employees created an atmosphere normalizing that making mistakes is a part of learning and their enjoyment of trying these exercise together is the goal. The elderly and municipal employees laughed by joking in the local dialect: "They are so easy, we can do it even faster," "You are so smart as your brain is 50 years younger than your actual age." Many exercises they do are quite complex, such as the exercise using the Stroop Effect, where the name of a color is printed in a color that is different from what is described in words. For example, the word, "yellow," is written in red. They read these 25 words aloud, and they tried another 25 words at an even faster speed. It appears quite cognitively challenging, but all the elderly tried with such an enthusiasm and some completed the exercise with great speed.

Municipal employees also gave their handmade calendar that allowed the elderly to mark the date they walked more than 30 minutes, napped more than 30 minutes, laughed more than 10 minutes, and talked with anyone outside of the house. The whole program was filled with laughter and smiles and there was no hierarchical relationship nor boundaries among municipal employees, elderly participants, and the volunteers. Municipal employees did not wear suits or formal clothes, but they wore clothes that are easy for them to do exercises and to blend in with the elderly they serve. If they wore something very formal and talk with them without any local dialects, it would have created hierarchical distance between them and the elderly.

In discussing the end of life options, municipal employees distributed their handmade handouts with illustrations and explanations that do not intimidate the elderly. They also used *kamishibai* (Japanese picture-story-show) to give an example that helps the elderly to understand what kind of information they need to know to process any paperwork related to getting public services. One of the handouts shows a population pyramid that illustrates that Kawanehonchō is Japan's future since the predicted population pyramid of Japan in 2060 resembles the population pyramid of Kawanehonchō in 2017. Many elderly laughed when the official employees told them that their town is the future town. They mentioned that, as the media recently reported, in the future, one elderly person supports another. In Kawanehonchō, it is already happening, since 1.1 elderly persons are supporting one elderly resident based on the statistics they provided. These charts made them realize that societies have changed demographically, and their behaviors should not be solely determined by *seken*, the normative expectation for family members to care for the elderly (see Chapter 1). Several elderly people whispered that we cannot rely just on families any longer based on their experiences, and others nodded in approval. Municipal employees agreed that it would be extremely difficult to solely rely on families, and they emphasized the importance of the elderly being informed and using services available to them. Everyone including the volunteers nodded deeply.

Municipal employees reassured their elderly audiences that the future is not to be feared, owing to the healthy longevity of the town and the supportive neighborhood. Municipal employees pointed out that there are four doctors available for house visits to allow the patients to spend their last moments at home at Kawanehonchō, which has as many doctors as the neighboring city. The handouts showed that, at Kawanehonchō, 25 percent of people passed away at home compared with 16 percent in Shizuoka Prefecture overall. Municipal employees showed a graph based on their interviews of 85 local people who lost an elderly family member. Many of the examples they used come from surveys they have conducted, making it more relatable. The graph showed that 54 out of the 85 decedents passed away at the hospital, 17 at home. Among those 17 respondents, four said that dying at the hospital could have been better for the elderly. A reason is that family members can spend more time talking with the elderly in their last moments instead of being stressed by taking on multiple caregiving roles. These voices appear to be really important for the elderly participating in the program to realize that dying at home may not always be the best option. They chatted with people sitting right next to them. A couple of minutes later, municipal employees have carefully and respectfully asked the elderly in local dialect, "Do you prefer to die at home?" Including volunteers, without any doubts, all of them raised their hands. Several elderly emphasized that they never want to leave their town and friends.

The handouts showed that, at this point, there are 17,694 beds at hospitals in Shizuoka Prefecture as of 2017; 10 years later 20,147 beds will be needed. Hospital beds will be expected to run short, and there is a great pressure for municipal governments to do something. Municipal employees illustrated their vision that their goal is for the elderly to be supported by not only family members but also people in the community, including care managers, doctors, nurses, pharmacists, helpers, and volunteers. Municipal employees explained that their role is to connect all together. In order for them to create the networks of support for the elderly, the employees reemphasize the importance of the elderly to be informed. In one of the handouts, illustrations emphasize the difficulty of family members in supporting the elderly, and the necessity of various people supporting the elderly (Figure 6.1). Several elderly people mentioned that they really appreciate the efforts municipal employees make in translating official documents to something they can understand and relate to.

Figure 6.1 Examples of Handout Used at the Genki Hatsuratsu Kyōshitsu

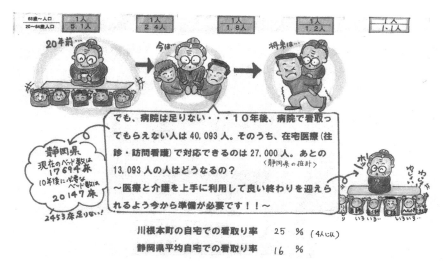

Note: This handout shows the significant changes in how many working-age people (20 to 64 years old) support one elderly person. It states that a bed shortage is expected and it emphasized the importance of the elderly to be informed so that they can be supported not only by family members, but also municipal workers, care managers, volunteers, helpers, doctors, nurses, pharmacists, and physical therapists. It states that being informed allows the elderly people to prepare for quality of life at the end-of-life period. It shows that 25 percent of the elderly in Kawanehonchō dying at home compared to 16 percent in Shizuoka Prefecture.

Municipal employees mentioned that there are attempts in other municipalities to strengthen the network of medical treatment and care, and some of these municipalities heavily rely on hospitals for establishing the network. However, as hospitals tend to consider a major indicator of success as the numbers of those being discharged, they may lack the time or incentive to foster formal and informal networks of out-patient care. In addition, hospitals do not have an in-depth understanding of the local elderly citizens and the community, as do the municipal employees who visit various districts and talk with the local elderly people, their families, and the volunteers.

Municipal employees explained to the elderly that in case they become hospitalized but want to be discharged, they can visit the hospital to talk with them and their family to understand what is needed for home care. Municipal employees can investigate whether they will be eligible for long-term care insurance. Such efficiency will allow the elderly to be smoothly assigned to the care manager who can coordinate what the elderly need after being discharged from the hospital (examples of such needs are visits from a pharmacist, nurse, or helper; or the loan of any equipment). It also allows the elderly patient and the family to start a discussion at the hospital with the care manager, doctor, nurses, and service providers on how the patient could continue to age in place. Municipal employees find that in-hospital planning is extremely important for the elderly patients to be supported by the local community, beyond the support from their families. A municipal employee shared a case of an elderly patient who was in the hospital with cancer. Learning that she could not recover, she eagerly hoped to go back to Kawanehonchō to spend her last moments at home. The municipal employee went to the hospital to talk with her, her family, and the doctor; they appointed a care manager who figured out all the necessary contacts and services for her to go home. In just over one hour, municipal employees talked with the patient and her family about informed consent and quality-of-life issues, and greatly helped them to make an informed decision. None of the elderly looked uncomfortable with listening to end-of-life options especially because they know the hard work municipal employees do. There is strong trust between municipal employees and the elderly participants in the program. Trust was built through offering these programs specifically designed to meet the needs of the elderly, and through transparency of municipal employees in sharing information they obtained from the central government in a way the elderly could understand and relate.

After the program, between 10:30 A.M. to 11 A.M., volunteers distributed tea and snacks and the elderly chatted about their lives and families. Having gone to the same school or sending their children to the same school, most of the elderly participants have known each other for decades, and they talk with one another as if they are brothers and sisters. Strong bonding social capital was easily observed through these conversations. Among these conversations, discussion about health was extremely popular. "I cannot eat much as I used to, so the doctor suggested me to have small meals for five times." "I had better results on the most recent check-ups. I think walking was the best treatment." "I saw on TV yesterday that taking blueberries will improve your eyes." Clearly, the elderly have high concerns about their health as many of them want to continue engaging in farm work or gardening.

Growing vegetables at home, a very popular activity here, is another popular conversation topic among the elderly. "Do you want to stop by my house after the salon? I have lots of cabbages." "I made some pickles from vegetables in my garden. I will stop by to give them to you later." Growing vegetables is not just for themselves to enjoy, but for them to share with their neighbors and friends. Vegetable exchange is a good example of cognitive social capital as it is not based on the rational calculation, but based on generalized reciprocity, good turns to be repaid at some unspecified time in the future. In rural towns like Kawanehonchō, there is a strong generalized reciprocity called *otagaisama*, referring to the importance of supporting one another without expecting any immediate return since everyone is in the same boat.

One of the major challenges in these programs is that some elderly men feel reluctant to participate because they believe these programs are for women. As the older adults historically received gender-segregated education, some of them, especially older men, feel more comfortable interacting with elderly people of the same gender. To encourage these elderly people to participate in the program, the municipal welfare office and the KCSW offer cooking classes and sporting events specifically targeted to men. Although cooking is considered women's work, offering cooking classes only for men makes it easier for them to enroll.

About three to five volunteers provide assistance to the program offered at their regional salon. The ages of these volunteers range from their 60s into their 70s; and they are busy during the program delivering snacks and/or cups of tea, cleaning up, and assisting the elderly needing support (e.g. bringing pencils, flipping pages, helping the elderly who need any assistance in exercises and crafts). They also help the program by organizing the yearly salon schedule, cleaning up the community center, identifying and recruiting the elderly to attend their salon, and informing the elderly about the next event. The volunteers' role is vital in smoothly running the program. Volunteers for each salon also provide useful information to municipal employees at the salon in regards to the elderly living alone since local volunteers are familiar with people living in their districts.

When the first author asked how they started volunteering, many of them responded that they consider themselves as participants, since they learn so much from the program. Few have raised issues of paid and unpaid volunteering, even though they have heard from others that volunteering needs to be paid if they are going to be absent from their paid work to participate. Several volunteers mentioned the challenge of finding successors, especially in the younger generations who have jobs. Volunteers mentioned that each salon is different. In some regional salons, the elders would like to invite lecturers; in others, the seniors prefer to take field trips. Organizing the budget and the yearly schedule and listening to the voices of the elderly are major tasks and are reasons why some salons are losing volunteers and becoming less active.

Carer's Café

Carer's Café (caretaker's café) targeted to caregivers is also organized by the municipal employees. This program is offered at several locations, but mainly at the public hot spring bath located in the Senzu district. A non-profit organization called Kawane Life also supports the program by providing transportation. The first author observed this program at the Sehira community center located at Shimonagao district in September, 2016. The program invited a lecturer to teach exercises; local residents from more than four districts attended the session. There were about 40 elderly caregivers, six of them being men. The program was supported by two NPO employees, three municipal employees, and three volunteers.

At 9 A.M., some elderly caregivers walked to the community salon, and others were provided transportation by their family or the municipal welfare office. Municipal employees greeted them and asked about any changes for them and their families while taking their blood pressure. The lecturer taught exercises for about one and half hours. All attending the program dressed nicely, enjoyed the conversation with small snacks and green tea, and chatted with their peers from other districts after the exercise program. After some tea and snacks, around 11 A.M., volunteers, municipal employees, and the elderly people helped each other to clean up the community center; and municipal employees smoothly grouped the elderly ones and assisted them into different public vehicles to take them home.

For the program offered at the Senzu district, when lectures are not on the program, the elderly participants can take a bath, and after that they chat with municipal employees and their friends about their life and concerns. One of the elderly participants in her 70s said, "Getting outside of home, talking with people other than family members, and having a place to let out my feeling of caring for a family member … I really appreciate these opportunities because I need them." Although this program is meant to give physical respite to caregivers, since most of the elderly residents are caregivers to their parents and spouses, there are many elderly people who participate in both programs at their regional salon and the Carer's café. Several elderly people told the first author that they are happy that they could participate in both to learn something new and meet old and new friends.

Another elderly participant in her 70s told the first author that she looks forward to seeing her grandchildren; but they live far away, and it is her *ikigai*, the purpose of life, to see and laugh with her friends by participating in the program like this. Another elderly person said: "I cannot wait for the next program. I mark the date and put it on the refrigerator so I will not forget." Another one said: "I sometimes cannot attend the program, but I do not want people in the group to forget about me so I will attend as much as I can." One of the elderly participants walks one kilometer to the community center and looks forward to learning something new.

Ikigai Day Service Center (IkiDay)

Ikigai Day Service centers/programs offer various activities for the elderly. There are three locations at Kawanehonchō. The first author observed two locations (Kaminagao and Okuizumi) in July, 2015, and September, 2016. There is usually one employee from the Kawanehonchō Council of Social Welfare (KCSW) in charge of the program, and one or two staff members who are public health nurses or care managers assist the elderly by taking blood pressure, answering any questions, and helping them set up paints and papers. About 15 to 20 elderly people, mostly women, participate in this day-program. The KCSW employees provide transportation for those who do not have it. Usually, the elderly participants go three days a week; they spend the whole day for US $3, and lunch is provided for an additional US $2.

Around 8:30 A.M. to 9:00 A.M., they arrive at the Ikigai Day Service center and talk with their friends; and from 9 A.M. to 12 P.M., they work at some activities, such origami, *chigirie* (Japanese torn paper art), calligraphy, exercising, and knitting (Figure 6.2). They invite a teacher who teaches these activities, and they are given some homework to do at the center. Some elderly adults work in a small group of four-to-five people; some in a big circle; and others on individual projects. Many of these activities are advanced and require complex hand movement.

Figure 6.2 The Elderly at the Ikigai Day Service Center

Photo provided by Kimiko Tanaka

There were elderly people in their 90s who completed various activities without any difficulty. One elderly woman in her 70s told the first author that she looks forward to giving what she made to her grandchildren. Another elderly woman took a calligraphy her friend worked on to show to her family members since it looked beautiful. Her friend said "It is so embarrassing!" but her face was full of smiles. When the elderly people worked on projects, they moved their hands while they talked to those sitting next to, or across from them. Many smiled and joked. One of them laughed and said to the group members: "The teacher is coming to take a look at our works of *chigi-rie*, and we are horrified." Others in the group laughed and suggested her to move her hands more quickly. Another one laughed and said: "My calligraphy is horrible!" Others told her "If yours is horrible, what is mine like?" They complained about how slow and imperfect their work is, but almost always the intent is to make others laugh and to reassure everyone that slowness and imperfection are all right as long as the activity is fun. Sitting in a big circle encourages the quiet elderly people to join the conversation.

Several elderly adults talked to the first author about her research. Knowing in advance that she would visit the facility, a couple of them brought a section of the local newspaper that discussed longevity in Kawanehonchō. The first author's research interest was featured in the municipal newsletter, and several elderly participants told her that they saw her in the local paper. Many asked her about aging in the U.S., and they were so surprised that American elderly tend not to visit their neighbors' homes like they do in Kawanehonchō. Several told her that they visit their neighbors almost every day to exchange home-grown vegetables. One asked: "How can you not to see the neighbor as there are more vegetables in my garden and I cannot eat them all?" At the same time, another elderly woman told the first author that her neighbor is so far away because so many people have moved out. She looks forward to lessening her isolation by coming to the center three days a week. Several told the first author how much they enjoy writing letters and sending their crafts to their friends and relatives. Many in their 70s, 80s and 90s who attend the center often read, write, and discuss various social issues with others.

The elderly greatly respect the KCSW employees who prepare all the activities and exercises. Employees often act as if they are the children or grand-children of the elderly participants, whom they ask about their vegetables, lands, local festivals, and cooking. The employees have great respect for their wisdom. All of the employees talked in local dialects, but they never talked with the elderly as if they were young children. The Japanese language has many verbs and nouns that convey honor. Employees changed their verb forms to show respect to the elders; at the same time, they were careful not to speak too formally, as it would create distance and hierarchy. When the elderly made suggestions in doing exercises and setting up chairs, employees took the stance of being students learning from the elderly. Infantilization is a serious affront in caring for the elderly, but the first author did not observe it at either facility she visited.

Konagai Salon Hustle

One of the biggest salons is called Konagai Salon Hustle, where the elderly meet once a month at the Konagai community center. Konagai, located relatively close to the train station, is one of the most populated areas in the town. A leader of the salon said that 10 years ago, the Konagai Salon Hustle was a small salon, but as word spread, more elderly people joined. There were about 40 elderly members, mostly women, and five volunteers gathering monthly at the salon when the first author visited in July, 2015. The KCSW helped in starting up the salon, and continues to support it in figuring out budgets and schedules. More commonly now, the elderly of this salon take the initiative in deciding the schedule and events. The salon is led by a local elderly woman who used to be the district welfare commissioner, called *minsei-iin*.[1] The respect received from others on her past experience enabled the group to be very autonomous and active in making decisions in regards to schedules, events, and setting up the community center. She knows everyone and their families extremely well as part of her experience as a district welfare commissioner; it has created a family-like environment. Her folder is filled with ideas obtained from professionals, books, and her friends. Their yearly schedule covers celebrating Japanese cultural events such as *setsubun*, the Spring festival in February, and *hinamatsuri*, the doll festival in March. These events allow the elderly to celebrate seasonal festivals, especially the ones who live alone or who do not have children to help them celebrate. They also do cheerleading at local sporting clubs at Kawane middle school to support the local community. They are so active that various media feature them in magazines and TV.

Most participants are women as in other salons; and a couple of elderly people told the first author that 70 is not considered old in this group. All of the elderly walk to the community center around 9 A.M. For all activities, four-to-five volunteers support the elderly, but they also blend in to participate in all the activities. The elderly and volunteers sing, dance, and play some games and do exercises for two hours. They play many group games, such as the singing game, where parts of childhood lyrics are written on cards, and they complete the song by finding partners. They also sit in a big circle and sing and clap to the beat of the music with the person sitting on the right. Volunteers make sure to see that no one is left out and to create the atmosphere that it is not a competition. Rather, it is a place of gathering, laughing, and talking with friends. They joke and laugh together that their brains and movements are younger than those in their 40s.

One of the elderly people told the first author that she walks more than 20 minutes to get to the community salon, and she looks forward to celebrating seasonal festivals with her friends. Another elderly woman said that she keeps the schedule handy and that she cannot wait for spring and fall day trips. Several elderly people told the first author that laughing really helps them to heal chronic illness. They can forget about pain when they keep their minds busy by laughing and talking with friends. Another elderly woman told the first author that she never tried karaoke and dancing before, but she tried it only because her friends tried it at the salon to sing together. She said she never thought that trying new things would be this exciting. During the tea time, they drink green tea with snacks; and with volunteers, the elderly clean up the community center after the gathering. The elderly people are proud of their local green tea; several commented that they do not drink brown tea, only green tea.

The elderly are not dependent at this salon; they are great contributors and participants to keep the program active and creative. Several elderly reported that it is challenging to try something new alone, but it is fun and encouraging if they try it together. They are surprised and glad that they have tried so many things they had not done before, such as cheerleading in front of local people and wearing costumes to dances. They had been working so hard on farming and raising their families; thus, working with their friends on some projects that are not based on duty and obligation is something very new to their lives. The great force behind them in running the program is their strong will to be part of the local community and their contentment in doing some activities together as an important part of *ikigai*, the purpose of life. In rural areas where there is no established system of paying membership fees to join classes, the importance of community membership is significant. Rather than feeling reluctant to be part of the tight community, the elderly growing up in the tight rural social network find that being part of the program is a significant purpose of life. The definition of collective efficacy, the ability of the community to collectively solve the problem, drives this salon, and everyone at the salon being so physically and cognitively healthy appears to be a positive outcome of such high collective efficacy in this neighborhood.

Quoits Tournament and the Exercise Group (Genki-up)

At a quoits tournament organized by the KCSW in September, 2016, there were more than 100 elderly participants (Figure 6.3). Each regional district has a senior quoits club, and there are more men than women participating in the tournament. They gathered at 9 A.M., and the event lasted until 3 P.M. Many groups claimed that they had practiced a lot for this tournament by meeting more frequently for longer hours. The first author sat with the Umetaka district quoits club, in which members in their mid-60s to early 70s have created a grass-roots group called Rakuyūkai. In this group, the younger elderly create the events, such as a sports day and a singing café. They created this informal salon where they can additionally meet with the elderly within the district and do some activities together without the need for a lot of paperwork for scheduling and budgeting. Some of them said that the major challenge of salons is that the people who attend these salons are the same; it can be difficult for new people, especially people in the mid-60s to early 70s, to join. Some of the people in their 60s and 70s have their parents in the salons, and the young-old children do not want to participate in the same activities as their parents. That could also deter recruiting volunteers for the salon. The need for young-old adults to have respite from their old-old parents is why the former created their own group, Rakuyūkai.

At the quoits tournament, a man in his late 60s asked the first author if she could spot anyone of the elderly attendees at the tournament who was overweight. He told her that most people living here had not worked in large firms

Figure 6.3 Quoits Tournament

Photo provided by Kimiko Tanaka

before their retirement, and that many had engaged in green tea, forestry, and local small industries. Thus, most of them rely on income from social security and savings. Many of them are not rich enough to travel to other prefectures or countries for leisure after retirement, and there are no expensive restaurants serving foods that are high in oil and fat. He was surprised to see obese people when he visited his children in urban towns, since it is difficult to find an obese person in Kawanehonchō. He also averred that the municipal office is excellent at keeping the elderly in shape by continuously reminding them of check-ups. Based on the results of check-ups, local doctors provide suggestions to improve their health conditions. The frequency of these check-ups is a motivation for many elderly to keep exercising.

Another man in his late 60s shared that many people attending today's tournament grow vegetables at home. He said: "Land is everywhere, since this is such an unpopulated place. Many of my friends are not wealthy like business managers who graduated from college and worked in cities and who have more retirement benefits and savings. Many elderly here do not buy vegetables because they have land, but also they are not wealthy like rich city people. But growing vegetables is good for our body, health, and mind."

One of the participants said: "I heard a saying that we should not laugh at the elderly since they are on the route we will walk to someday. So helping them is the same as helping yourself into the future." Several elderly people shared their excitement about local festivals in which they used to actively participate; but now it is physically difficult for them to participate as they used to. Now their children are leading these local festivals, and their neighbors are helping them because all are under the protection of the local deity. Another volunteer told me that they weed the local streets because the other elderly people cannot do it. Making the street clean will benefit everyone in the community. Generalized reciprocity, *otagaisama*, was honored and alive in their everyday conversations.

The first author also observed the exercise group called Genki-up in October, 2016. Eleven people from their mid-60s to mid-80s meet once a week in the morning for an hour to do exercises at the gymnasium next door to the municipal office. The exercise instructor is a woman who came to Kawanehonchō to take this job and then married a local man. She said that she has learned names and dialects and uses them a lot to blend in. A woman in her mid-60s who participates in the exercise program also moved to Kawanehonchō because of her marriage at least 40 years ago, but she still feels that she is not fully blended into those who have lived in Kawanehonchō all their lives. She sees a distinction between those who grew up and lived most of their life in the town versus others, who are regarded as outsiders. She said it does not mean that natives are not welcoming newcomers. She emphasized how kind they were in welcoming and teaching her about local festivals and folklore. She meant to describe the richness of the culture and environment which makes the local people distinctive. Friendships of more than 40, 50, and 60 years were frequently observed at various activities. Friendship of such long duration are quite different from the friendship solely based on hobbies and club memberships. A person knowing not only about the friend but also his or her families well is quite common in this town.

Four years ago, there were only a few people participating in Genki-up, possibly being suspicious of activities offered by an instructor from the outside. As they got to know the instructor and told others about the program, the number of participants in the exercise group gradually grew to 11 in 2016.

They do yoga and Pilates at an intermediate level, and they do various exercises that require them to use their cognitive ability fully. The instructor tells them to move their hands and legs right and left for certain periods of time. According to the instructor, she does not push the elderly since the strict obedience to teachers enforced on them during their childhood may cause them to overwork. However, the instructor finds that her elderly students learn the routines quickly and request new routines. One of the participants said, she drives to the gymnasium to participate, so gets to meet people outside her district as a bonus. According to another participant, Kawanehonchō is a very tight community, but the residents are open to others. After all, forestry, the green tea industry, and the hot springs have historically attracted outsiders who support the economic vitality of the town.

Summary

One of the unique strengths of Kawanehonchō appears to be the layering of the social networks. Municipal employees, employees of the KCSW, local volunteers, and the elderly participants support various programs and grassroots organizations, which allow the local senior citizens multiple points of entry. The elderly can participate in more than one program per week, and the town creates a loop to avoid social isolation. For many elderly, participating in these preventive programs became *ikigai,* the purpose of life. Urban elderly tend to work as employees of corporations that have certain dates for retirement, allowing them to prepare for lifestyles after their retirement. There are various options for people of all ages to seek and join classes they are interested in, and many are based on paid membership. On the other hand, rural elderly tend to continue working in forestry or farming, which does not require them to retire at a certain age. Thus, many local people do not get used to the idea of applying and joining for the membership. Various programs offered through the local public, private, and grassroots organizations allow them to feel connectedness to friends and neighbors, which makes it easier for the elderly to join and continue participating in these activities. The cost of participating is free, if not trivial compared to fees for joining membership in gyms or cultural classes in urban areas.

Furthermore, in rural towns like Kawanehonchō, there is a strong generalized reciprocity called *otagaisama*, referring to the importance of supporting one another without expecting any immediate return. The elderly who are physically capable set up chairs for the elderly who are not; the elderly who are hearing-disabled get oral interpretation from hearing-abled peers sitting beside them. Several times, the elderly tried to tell the first author about their children at tea time, but they could not recall their children's ages. The elderly sitting beside another elder helped by saying: "Your older daughter is __ years old since she is a year older than my daughter, and your second daughter is __ years old because she is a year younger than the first one." Several volunteers also use the word, *otagaisama*, in explaining their contributions to the community.

At an early stage of the research, one of the elderly in Kawanehonchō kindly offered to accompany the first author to several facilities for the elderly and introduce her as a reliable person of good will who was coming to Kawanehonchō for academic research. He said: "My daughter is also a researcher and she was kindly welcomed and supported at her research site, so by my helping you, I will return the kindness my daughter received." After observing the programs, since it is difficult to find easily available transportations in the town, the author was asked by several participants if she knows how she can get back. Generalized reciprocity, reflected in the concept of *otagaisama*, was deeply rooted in the community and observed at these programs.

Finally, the elderly people in Kawanehonchō greatly benefit from these programs. These programs not only reduce the feeling of social isolation and increase the health literacy among the elderly participants, but also strengthen the collective efficacy of the neighborhood. Observations of these programs also suggest that knowing what to, and how to, prepare for aging in place and having a reliable community provide rich structural capital and contribute to healthy aging, more an important factor than individual socioeconomic levels. To further understand people supporting and creating these programs, we will discuss the findings from the interviews with various leaders in Kawanehonchō in the next chapter.

∼ Seven ∼

Interviews with Local Leaders

At Kawanehonchō, there are various public and private organizations providing programs for those who are classified as not needing care but needing to avoid social isolation and to remain healthy. For those who are assessed as requiring care ("requiring care levels 1 to 5") by the municipal welfare office, there are daycare and long-term care facilities. For those who were classified as "requiring support levels 1 and 2" there are day-care services. (See Chapter 2 for detailed explanations of these levels). The offices and services are run by municipal employees, Kawanehonchō Council of Social Welfare (KCSW) employees, care managers, salon leaders, local volunteers, salon and senior club leaders, district welfare commissioners (*minsei-iin*), and staff from non-profit organizations. Because it is important to know multiple viewpoints, the first author met fifteen people in these roles and interviewed them between 20 and 50 minutes in an open-ended format. She asked them to describe important social factors about aging in the town in July 2015, and September and October 2016. Below are common themes that appeared through the interviews.

Otagaisama

Otagaisama, a strong sense of reciprocity and trust within social networks, is a keyword observed by the elderly participating in the program and those who support the program (see Chapter 6). The mayor, municipal employees, salon leaders, district welfare commissioners, and volunteers frequently used the word *otagaisama* to affirm that their elderly residents have supported the town and deserve repayment by means of eldercare services. All of the community leaders and volunteers affirmed that they support the elderly as citizens with a strong feeling of *otagaisama*. Such a strong sense of reciprocity in the community is developed through the everyday life of interacting with one another as if one big family and supporting the local festival in each district.

Norms of reciprocity were also used to explain why they support others. A former district welfare commissioner told the first author that neighbors visited his house to talk about their or their children's problems. After listening to them carefully, he gave suggestions and directed them to the right person without making them feel intimidated. Because his house is very close to the local train station, it has become a place for the people to gather. He never received any payment from people who consulted him. He believes that he, as a leader, should help others in the neighborhood. He said, it is truly *otagaisama*.

A salon leader mentioned the green tea industry as an example of *otagaisama*. Green tea became the local beverage of hospitality of this town. When green tea farming became a large part of the community economy, the green tea farms spurred ways to enact community reciprocity. One of the older volunteers mentioned that in the past there was a school break for young children to help handpick green tea leaves to help local green tea farmers. Today, local schools teach a tea service to their students, and invite the tea farmers to teach the students how to cultivate and make green tea. Green tea has connected and enhanced mutual reciprocity through exchanges of labor, knowledge, and appreciation. People served green tea anywhere the first author visited, and tea time created time, communal space, appreciation, and conversation. A volunteer in her 70s said, "Not only female seasonal workers who migrated to pick leaves for green tea, but also the town used to have so many outsiders for the forestry and other business such as Chubu Electric Power, Inc." Areas surrounded by trees may make people imagine the town is isolated from others, but the town has historically always welcomed outsiders. The success behind tourism is not only the natural resources, but also *omotenashi*, the hospitality of volunteers and local people to welcome others that has been sustained over generations through the spirit of *otagaisama*.

Several leaders pointed out that many green tea farms stretched across mountain slopes requiring both manual labor and machinery, and many of these farms lack a younger generation to carry on the physical and managerial work. Today, the municipal office and the Kawanehonchō Council of Social Welfare (KCSW) are bridges between the elderly who cannot frequently take care of their green tea fields by themselves and those who can help them for a fixed, reasonable hourly fee. Their pride towards the history of the green tea industry and the spirit of *otagaisama* is a drive to make this community active and to beautify the scenery of this town. If the town loses more people, it will become more difficult to maintain the green tea farms and to continue attracting tourists to the scenery.

Local Festivals

The Mayor and the volunteers at salons emphasized the importance of local festivals in developing the feeling of *otagaisama* throughout the life course. Each district of Kawanehonchō has a shrine where local festivals allow local people to collectively thank the gods protecting their land. Older residents teach younger ones the songs, dances, and appropriate roles of seniors in carrying on the festival's traditions. It is becoming extremely difficult to pass on these local festivals in some districts due to depopulation by losing local people who have participated in the festival since they were children. One of the salon leaders said, "This town has opportunities for the old to pass on their skills and stories to the younger generations through various events at festivals and local schools. Some students in middle school and high school visit elder homes to learn the importance of care. Students in elementary school learn how to make local crafts and listen to regional folktales of Kawanehonchō from the elderly at events at schools. Many leaders emphasized that they want to pass on these resources to repay the community." Another salon leader pointed out: "The problem is that there is no good balance between the young and the old, not enough young people to assume leadership roles. Without passing on these festivals to younger residents, the culture of *otagaisama* could disappear."

Emphasis on the Life Course Perspective in Providing Care for the Elderly with Dementia

A care manager at the day-care facility mentioned that many of the elderly there suffer from dementia at varying levels. She does not know many of the elderly, and their disability does not allow them to describe their needs clearly. In that case, she carefully looks through their folders that contain descriptions of their previous occupations and lifestyles reported by family members and the memos written by employees when they interviewed family members upon registration. One day, one of the elderly men suffering from dementia looked sad. The information in the folder said he loved walking, and it was his daily routine before his level of dementia accelerated. So she took him for a walk around the facility, and they admired cherry blossoms. She was surprised at how relaxed he was after they came back to the facility. She told the first author that it is difficult to walk with him every day because she must care for other elderly residents, but she takes him for a walk when her time allows. She also mentioned that many elderly residents in Kawanehonchō helped out on green tea farms when they were growing up. Even if they cannot remember anything from their childhood, their eyes shine with excitement and their bodies remember all the movements to pick green tea leaves when they go on a field trip to a tea farm.

Another care manager at a different day-care facility said she had known some of the elderly since childhood. She emphasized the importance of not generalizing care. Because she has more than 20 years of experience in caring for the elderly, she is teaching herself and others the need to tailor care to the individual. In the past, the day care facility was mostly occupied by elderly people who had been self-employed workers or farmers. Today, the elderly are from a greater variety of occupational backgrounds. The variety has greatly changed the way caregivers must interact with the elderly, because their occupational history strongly influences the way they behave and interact, even in the presence of dementia. The care manager emphasized the importance of looking into the eyes of the elderly, a time-consuming challenge due to her busy schedule. One time, she was talking with an elderly woman with dementia and used eye contact to send the non-verbal message that she was really interested in the story. Then the elderly person started to talk about how to make pickles in such detail and excitement. Interacting with people with progressive dementia, she finds that among elderly people with it, their long-term memories seem to last longer than short-term memories. An employee working at the Ikigai Day Service center (IkiDay) also mentioned that eye contact encourages the elderly to open up about what they recall about their past lives. He was amazed with their cognitive ability to talk about their jobs and childhood.

All the care providers emphasized the importance of looking at the life course of the elderly. Because the elderly's lifelong contributions to the local community are well-respected, it appeared to influence their enthusiasm in listening to their stories about green tea farming, gardening, and making pickles. Not just having someone to listen, but having someone interested in listening to their life stories, appears to make a difference in the quality of care.

Taking a Walk in Other People's Shoes

Municipal employees emphasized the importance of visiting and participating in programs so that the elderly can talk with local people face-to-face. The goal is definitely not to create a hierarchical relationship where the municipal employees tell the elderly what to do based on the manual. A municipal employee believes that hierarchical relationships will create eldercare programs insensitive to individual or collective needs. One of her goals in visiting each salon is to create an atmosphere that makes it comfortable for the elderly to talk about any issues and opinions. Since she is senior to other employees, it is especially important that she takes at least two other people from the municipal welfare office with her to visit each salon. It allows her to hear the messages from the perspectives of her younger employees, as well as from the elderly people themselves and the regional volunteers. She emphasized that it is best practice to listen to local people to create programs for the elderly, since local people know best about the area and its residents. She said: "Programs cannot be designed by people who have never visited Kawanehonchō."

Many elderly in Kawanehonchō exercise frequently through salon activities, senior clubs, and growing vegetables. There are not many restaurants or convenience stores, so they do not have the habit of purchasing high-fat food for their convenience. Recently the Japanese government and media recommended the importance of reducing cholesterol to remain healthy. If the elderly follow the recommendation and change their diet to reduce cholesterol, it could influence their health negatively, such as causing malnutrition. For these elderly people, reducing the amount of grilled meat, which contains fat, could negatively influence their physical health, since some dietary fat is necessary. Since municipal workers know elderly adults will follow guidelines, the former need to be very careful in giving information in regards to health in visiting salons.

Furthermore, the municipal employees mentioned that she visits the elderly who are socially isolated to listen to their voices and their families. Based on listening to their voices, she felt that they thought their lives were over because they had been assessed as needing support for the activities of daily living (ADLs). She encourages the elderly not to think of aging as one pattern of downward movement. She emphasized: "It is important to recognize that aging is not one-way, and aging should be recognized as a way for them to maintain their physical and cognitive level or to improve it." Not only listening to the elderly and younger co-workers, municipal employees hold meetings with the KCSW employees, salon leaders, volunteers, and the local people in developing and modifying programs. Carer's Café is a successful example of such collaboration.

A care manager at the daycare center said, "People here have a strong dialect, and outsiders may find it rough. But if we talk in formal Japanese to the elderly, they will not clearly understand what we are saying." Non-profit organization employees and municipal employees also emphasized the importance of the local dialect in communicating with the elderly so that the programs are developed to fit the local context and distributed to the elderly in the format they find familiar. None of these leaders except the mayor wear suits. They wear gym clothes that make it easier for them to move around and talk with the elderly. Wearing suits is important for a mayor who represents the town to outsiders, but informal clothing helps municipal employees or volunteers to place themselves on a more equal, less intimidating position with the elderly people.

Importance of Not Making Assumptions

The mayor, the care managers at the elder homes, the daycare facilities, and the municipal offices; and the salon leaders emphasized the importance of not making assumptions. Kawanehonchō is a rural town, so people assume that it is not ideal for raising academically successful children. However, the low teacher-student ratio allows teachers to spend more time with individual students. In addition to beautiful nature for canoeing, fishing, bicycling, and paragliding, local elderly residents and volunteers visit schools to teach crafts and stories that have been passed down through the generations, and that enriches children's minds. Medical expenses are free up to high school. They expressed their concerns that the perception that people could gain a better quality of education in cities is one reason why younger adults with children do not settle in Kawanehonchō.

A senior club leader also pointed out that people are biased against rural areas, although they positively perceive the word "resort." He asked, "What is the difference between Kawanehonchō and a resort?" Many volunteers emphasized the town is easier to live in since the cost of land is much cheaper than in cities, plus the town offers the medical benefits for raising children. One of the volunteers pointed out that an international software corporation, Zoho, which has its home office in India, opened up a satellite office in Kawanehonchō. She hopes that more companies, especially in the information-technology (IT) industry, realize the benefits of living in this town. In order to make that happen, she believes it is necessary to break down negative stereotypes about rural towns.

A manager at the long-term care facility pointed out the importance of not making assumptions in interacting with the elderly. One of the care managers assumed that an elderly man who had lost his vision could not enjoy fireworks. But he was enjoying the event by imagining the fireworks with the sound. A KCSW employee pointed out that sometimes he does not feel that he is actually assisting elderly people because of their excellent physical and cognitive level. A municipal employee also pointed out that the line between the elderly people and the caregiver is blurred, since caregivers and volunteers are aging, sometimes faster than the elderly participants in the program. "Assumptions can be dangerous," another care manager at a daycare facility emphasized. Since she also manages home-care services, she visits various elderly people's homes to care for and talk with them. She is concerned that the media spotlighted Kawanehonchō as a town full of healthy and active elderly people not needing nursing homes. However, rapid depopulation left elderly people living alone in remote areas, and some are so lonely that they hope to move to the elder care facility regardless of their disability status. What younger people find to be "close" to the neighbor's house, the elderly may view as "distant."

"Not everyone nor the families are the same. Not everyone has family members frequently visiting him or her at the nursing home," said another care manager at the long-term care facility. She mentioned that there are families who do not even come to the annual meeting while there are elderly people who come and visit their spouse at the facility every day. The employees encourage families to visit at least twice a year to change the clothes in the closets for the elderly. This facility has a hospice room where families can keep vigil over a dying elderly relative. The staff regards the end-of-life directives as important to obtain from the elderly upon admission to the facility to insure that their last wishes are known while they can still express them. Many families asked the facility to let the relative stay at the facility, not at a hospital, in the final days before death. Sometimes the younger relatives have a contrary opinion to that of their senior relatives, and it can change over time. That is why younger relatives are encouraged to visit their senior relatives more than once a year. "Every family is different," she emphasized.

A salon leader and a municipal employee both expressed concern about Kawanehonchō's ranking as having one of the longest life expectancies in the prefecture, since it may create performance pressures that could result in a heavy focus on quantitative measures of "success." Some salons do not allow the media to visit since it distracts the elderly, and their gathering is not for the media. "We gather the local elderly for the local elderly," the salon leader emphasized. Various media have featured Kawanehonchō as the town full of healthy elderly people, listing possible causes as green tea, diet, and daily exercise, and creating assumptions about the causes of longevity. Some local leaders showed appreciation that the town is featured as it helps to revitalize it, but at the same time they are cautious to protect the elderly.

Concern for the Future

Mayors, volunteers, salon leaders, and care managers all raised their concern for the future since they have seen changes in the town. "Kids were everywhere, but now it is hard to find them." Such voices were heard from everyone the first author interviewed. Currently, there are four elementary schools. Honkawane Elementary School emerged when two schools were consolidated in 2006, but these two schools were in turn the result of consolidating seven elementary schools. This elementary school had only 44 students in 2020. There have been voices for and against consolidating elementary schools further due to the declining enrollment and a need to save public revenue. One of the salon leaders stated: "We lose the future if we lose more children. We lose children if we lose more schools. Local festivals cannot be passed down to future generations if the town continues to lose people. Luckily in our town, the local festival takes place since children come back for the summer vacation. But as the absolute number of the children decreases in this town, it is becoming more difficult to pass on the traditions." These leaders are not just focusing on supporting the elderly, but also on the youth for Kawanehonchō to avoid further merger.

Summary

Local leaders' perceptions of how they support the elderly are based on the spirit of *otagaisama,* and the great emphasis on listening to voices of the people involved in programs and services. A high degree of collective efficacy in the community appears to make them consciously or unconsciously emphasize listening as the important skill during the interview. None of the leaders ever infantilized the elderly when describing in the interviews how they interact with them. A couple inferred the importance of not making simplistic assumptions behind longevity in the town solely based on individual level variables such as green tea intake and daily exercise. To further understand healthy agers in Kawanehonchō, we distributed a survey to the elderly participating in the programs provided by Kawanehonchō municipal welfare office and KCSW. Survey results are discussed in the next chapter.

∼ Eight ∼

Understanding Characteristics of the Elderly Participants

To gain further insights, from September to November, 2016, we distributed a survey at three district centers where the elderly gather to participate in programs offered by the Kawanehonchō municipal welfare office and the Kawanehonchō Council of Social Welfare (KCSW). The population size of these districts varied as well as the geographical location. Recently, there are increasing scams targeting the elderly, and the elderly have been told to be careful in responding to any requests. In fact, on the day the first author visited one of the district community centers, municipal employees collaborating with the employees from KCSW were announcing a special session on how to prevent elders from being scammed. Since the elderly trust the people at the municipal welfare office and KCSW, our decision to distribute the survey through these offices provided efficiency, trust, and a high response rate.

The employees at these places provided permission to distribute the survey and introduced the first author as a researcher to the elderly people. After consulting with the municipal employees, we decided to shorten the survey, since it would have been physically demanding for the elderly to complete many questions after an activity. As a result, the questionnaire took an average of 20 minutes to complete. At one location where KCSW offers the program, about half of the elderly needed assistance in reading the questions and marking their responses. In such cases, the first author interviewed them and checked the responses on their behalf. For two other locations, most elderly could complete the survey without any assistance. At all locations, some elderly talked with the first author to provide more feedback. At two locations where KCSW offers the program, all the elderly participated in the survey. At one location where the municipal government offers the program, a total of four elderly people decided not to participate in the survey. As a result, a total of 58 elderly people participated in the survey.

Table 8.1 summarizes the survey results. As it has been discussed before, the vast majority of participants were women (in fact, more than 80 percent). At one location, all the participants were women. Activities offered at this location were mostly physical exercises and such crafts as calligraphy and origami art. The activities may discourage elderly men, who may be too shy for cultural reasons to hold or clap hands with elderly women. Since there were not many male participants, their presence was greatly appreciated by others.

Table 8.1 Descriptive Statistics of Elderly Participants in Programs in Kawanehonchō

Variables	Frequency	Percentage
Sex		
Men	10	17.2
Women	48	82.8
Marital Status		
Never	2	3.4
Married	18	31.0
Spouse deceased	30	51.7
Living separately from the spouse	2	3.4
No response	6	10.3
Living Arrangement		
Living alone	18	31.0
Only with a spouse	8	13.8
Spouse and children	22	37.9
Only with a child	1	1.7
Others	9	15.5

Housing

Own house	55	94.8
Rent	2	3.4
Others	1	1.7

Living Standard

Well	3	5.2
Somewhat well	4	6.9
Normal (*futsuu*)	48	82.8
Little hard	2	3.4
Hard	1	1.7

Income

From work and Social Security	1	1.7
Social Security Only	57	98.3

Occupation

Currently working	3	5.2
Retired	35	60.3
Never worked	17	29.3
Missing	3	5.2

Social Participation

Neighborhood association	13	22.4
Programs offered through municipal office and/or KCSW	58	100.0
Volunteer work	1	1.7
Sporting/hobby club	11	19.0
Local festival	8	13.8

Neighborhood relations

Visiting each other's house	45	77.6
People visit my house	4	6.9
Just talk outside casually	6	10.3
Just greeting	2	3.4
Almost no relationship	1	1.7

How you think of the neighbor

Easy because of no thick relations	10	17.2
Lonely because of weakened relations	8	13.8
Easy because of thick relations	36	62.1
Tired because of thick relations	3	5.2
Missing	1	1.7

Helped by neighbor this year	**31**	**53.4**
Emergency support	4	6.9
Checking-up safety/health	12	20.7
Asking for opinion/suggestion	13	22.4
Assistance in going out	7	12.1
Asking for any assistance	10	17.2
Helping out with household chores	10	17.2

Helping neighbor this year	**25**	**43.1**
Emergency support	3	5.2
Checking-up safety/health	10	17.2
Asking for opinion/suggestion	11	19.0
Assistance in going out	4	6.9
Asking for any assistance	8	13.8
Helping out with household chores	5	8.6

Interaction with young people	**38**	**65.5**
Through Family members	12	20.7
Through activities	31	53.4
Staying alone		
During daytime	17	29.3
During nighttime	8	13.8
Almost never	25	43.1
Almost always (day and night)	7	12.1
Missing	1	1.7
What you consider important in thinking of relationship with neighbors		
Greeting	54	93.1
Participate in recycling	29	50.0
Participate in local festivals	43	74.1
Cleaning the neighborhood	30	51.7
Supporting childcare	6	10.3
Supporting the elderly and people with disability	8	13.8
Participate in emergency drills	39	67.2
Supporting folk culture	24	41.4
Nothing in particular	1	1.7
Things you do to keep you healthy		
Walking/Exercising	46	79.3
Eating breakfast	51	87.9
Participating in activities	43	74.1
Working	27	46.6
Communicating with others	38	65.5
Writing/calculating	18	31.0

Care assessment

No	50	86.2
Yes (support 1)	5	8.6
Missing	3	5.2

Last check-up

Less than a month	21	36.2
Less than half a year	19	32.8
Less than a year	11	19.0
Not for over a year	4	6.9
Missing	3	5.2

Seeing doctors for physical problems

Yes	31	53.4
No	22	37.9
Missing	5	8.6

ADLs/IADLs (N and % of those who responded not difficult)

Cleaning	36	62.1
Carrying a shopping bag	39	67.2
Climbing stairs	29	50.0
Bending	38	65.5
Walking	37	63.8
Changing clothes	51	87.9
Calling	50	86.2

Self-rated health

Very good	10	17.2
Good	14	24.1
Average	29	50.0
Below average	4	6.9
Missing	1	1.7

Average Number of Sons (SD)   1.32 (1.06)

Average Number of Daughters (SD)   1.14 (1.03)

Co-residence

Living with the daughter[1]   4

Living with the son[2]   24

Living with the eldest son[3]   20

Living with unmarried eldest son[4]   5

Presence of unmarried children

Unmarried son[5]   13

Unmarried daughter[6]   4

	Men	**Women**
Age	83.4 (SD=6.35)	82.96 (SD=4.91)
Years of living at Kawanehonchō	83.4 (SD=6.35)	76.63 (SD=13.96)
N	10	48

1. Out of 58 respondents, 4 respondents left this section blank and 17 respondents said that they do not have any daughters.
2. Out of 58 respondents, 4 respondents left this section blank and 13 responded that they do not have any sons.
3. Out of 58 respondents, 4 left this section blank and 13 responded that they do not have any sons.
4. Out of 58 respondents, 5 left this section blank and 13 responded that they do not have sons.
5. Out of 58 respondents, 10 left this section blank and 13 responded that they do not have any sons.
6. Out of 58 respondents, 13 left this section blank and 17 responded that they do not have any daughters.

The average age of both male and female participants was 83 years. For men, the age of participants ranged from 75 to 94 years old. Although it is impossible to generalize based on a sample of 10 men participating the program, the average numbers of years they had lived in Kawanehonchō was exactly the same as their average age. Evidently none of these male participants had left home since birth.

For women, the age of the respondents ranged from 72 to 93 years old, and the years of living in Kawanehonchō ranged from 40 to 92. It suggested that some women had moved to the town through marriage, and that some had married someone from neighboring districts. The descriptive statistics suggest that many elderly participants in the program have known each other for a very long time. It creates a sense of comfort to the elderly (bonding social capital); at the same time, it limits interacting with those whose backgrounds are different at these programs (bridging social capital).

As these programs specifically target the elderly who do not need immediate long term care insurance (LTCI), most elderly participants in these programs were physically healthy. The majority of the elderly had never been assessed by government employees for requiring care or support (See Chapter 1 for detailed explanation of LTCI and the levels of care and support). Only five elderly adults were assessed as "requiring support level 1," that they needed partial support in daily living activities such as standing up. In assessing the respondents' activities of daily living (ADLs) and instrumental activities of daily living (IADLs), a majority replied with confidence that they had no problem cleaning, carrying a shopping bag, climbing up stairs, bending, walking, changing clothes, and calling their family and friends (Table 8.1). Several elderly respondents pointed out that they do not frequently carry a shopping bag because they do not frequently go shopping; stores are miles away. Although it is impossible to generalize for all the elderly participants from all the districts of this town, the fact is that the average age of elderly participants is so high, but that the majority have no issues with ADLs. Apparently, healthy aging could be achieved in rural depopulated areas without the advanced hospitals. Plausibly, collective efficacy and social capital benefited the health of the rural elderly people in Kawnehonchō.

In terms of marital status, most respondents were widows or widowers (51.7 percent), and nearly one-third of the elderly (31 percent) were living alone (Table 8.1). It showed the effectiveness of these programs in identifying and helping them to avoid social isolation. Indeed, several elderly respondents told the first author that they wanted to avoid the social isolation from living alone. One participant said that she had started participating in the program after being contacted by municipal employees. Another participant mentioned that she did not realize it was such fun to talk with people rather than staying home alone until she joined the program. At the same time, several respondents reported that they really looked forward to some weekends when their children visit their house and provide transportation to purchase the food and clothing they want. One of the participants said with excitement: "My daughter works in the city. I always look forward to traveling with her when she is on vacation." Meanwhile, these gatherings are really helpful in avoiding social isolation. For a majority of them, the program provided by the Kawanehonchō municipal office and/or KCSW is the only group in which they participate (Table 8.1).

Influenced by the *ie* system, the system of primogeniture (see Chapter 1), at least 23 respondents live with their child. Nine respondents checked "others" for the question on living arrangements. Several commented that they were not sure whether their children living in their house for a couple of days a week or over weeks counts as co-residents. One respondent mentioned that her daughter can afford to stay in her house for a longer period of time because her grandchildren are all independent. Another elderly adult said her son stays at her home every weekend. Thus, the number of respondents living with children could be greater than 40 percent.

Among 24 respondents who checked that they live with their son, 20 of these were the eldest; and five of these eldest sons were also unmarried. Thirteen respondents who answered they had at least one son checked that they had an unmarried son; four respondents checked that they had at least one unmarried daughter. These numbers could be underestimated as the first author could sense the sensitivity of this question, due to the possibility of stigma attached to being unmarried. It illustrates another demographic problem Japan faces - a trend of increasing numbers of single men and women.

In terms of living standards, many respondents told the first author it was "*futsuu*," meaning normal. Most respondents were retired, living in the house they owned, and solely on a pension. Since most residents own their homes (94.8 percent), they grow their own vegetables; and several elderly proudly stated that they never needed to purchase vegetables. In fact, when the elderly are en route home from the senior center, some stop by each other's homes to exchange surplus vegetables. An elderly woman in her early 70s proudly mentioned that she had never bought vegetables because she had always gotten them from her friends and from her garden. Another elderly woman said: "I never needed to learn how to grow vegetables by the books. My grandparents and parents always grew vegetables. We helped them pick and eat them." As the majority of the respondents considered their living standard to be neither well nor hard, socioeconomic status appeared to be homogeneous among the respondents and not creating differences in healthy longevity.

Almost all the elderly participants (93.1 percent) considered greetings to be important in their relationships with neighbors. Other popular salient interactions were participation in the local festivals (74.1 percent), emergency drills (67.2 percent), cleaning the neighborhood (51.7 percent), and recycling (50 percent). The importance they attached to keeping the neighborhood clean, safe, and active suggested a high degree of informal social control.

A high level of collective efficacy also explained why Kawanehonchō had an extremely low crime rate. According to the municipal statistical record of 2017, the rate of crime was one case per 33.1 days (Kawanehonchō Office 2017). Various media reported that the increase in crimes, such as shoplifting by Japanese seniors, was partly explained by social isolation (Hu 2016). A lack of senior crime in Kawanehonchō showed the importance of social cohesion and informal social control in not only making these seniors feel secure from harm but also preventing senior crimes caused by social isolation.

A majority of respondents (77.6 percent) mentioned that their neighborhood relations consist mainly of visiting each other's house. Only one respondent remarked that she had almost no relationship with her neighbors. She commented on the questionnaire that it is not that she does not want to interact with her neighbors, but that the five households in her district are geographically far apart. For her, the shuttle service KCSW provides allows her to make new friends and talk with and consult with municipal employees three times a week. A majority of neighbors positively value their strong neighborhood relationship. Three elderly checked on the statement that they are tired of strong neighborhood relationships. One of them who is living alone came to the first author to comment that, "tired of the strong neighborhood relationship" is not exactly how she feels, but she checked that response because she feels guilty and reluctant about not being able to participate in her neighborhood association due to her age while others send their spouse or children to these meetings. Eight elderly people mentioned that they felt lonely due to weakened relationships. Several elderly people mentioned that they feel especially sad about weakened ties to younger generations due to depopulation. A majority of people (53.4 percent) responded that these programs provide them with welcomed opportunities to interact with younger generations since students occasionally visit some of these programs.

In regards to helping others or being helped by neighbors, reflecting their age, more than half of the respondents reported that they were helped by their neighbors this year. Several elderly participants said it was part of their daily conversation to talk about their health and families when they saw each other. One elderly woman enthusiastically shared that she was immediately assisted when she fell and screamed at her front door in the evening. She was so glad to have a neighbor who made good decisions, which really shortened her recovery. Another elderly woman mentioned that her neighbor will help her take down laundry when it rains, and several said their neighbors held bags for them. Based on years of interactions between neighbors, people would sometimes leave gifts such as vegetables near the front door of an absent neighbor without having to leave a note of explanation. Several elderly people emphasized that they do not want to leave this town because they would not have people who would help them like people in this town. These results suggest a high degree of social cohesion and informal social control in the neighborhood: that people are willing to exchange help with their neighbors and considered themselves as residents of a close-knit neighborhood. While many of the elderly respondents frequently visited neighbors and helped others like themselves, several commented to the first author that it was becoming hard to do so nowadays: there are no longer many households in their district.

Several elderly participants asked the first author an inquiry about the survey question of when they experience being alone. The choices were: 1. "during day time"; 2. "during night time"; and 3. "almost never." Seven participants commented on the questionnaire or told the first author that they are almost always alone when they do not participate in the program. An elderly woman commented to the first author that she was almost always alone day and night on dates when she does not participate in the program. She truly appreciated these gatherings where she could talk and laugh with people, which became her *ikigai*, the purpose of life. Another elderly woman who visited the program for the first time mentioned that she came because she was alone all day. At first, she looked uncomfortable, but about half hour later, she was in the circle working on the crafts with others. Others welcomed her and asked her various questions in seeking whether they know her friends, relatives, or neighbors. Once they figured out several people they both knew, the conversation became more casual. Friendship does not have to be built over the life course, for it can be built through finding mutual friends. In fact, nearly 75 percent of the elderly responded that participating in these activities helped them to remain healthy, and over 65 percent reported that talking with others had that effect.

A majority of the elderly had seen their home doctors within the past year. Several elderly credited the municipal office for reminding them multiple times to get their health check-ups. Their frequent visits to their doctors pressured them to remain healthy. Half rated their health as average. There were so many elderly who were physically and cognitively healthy based on activities they performed in these programs. It appeared some elderly were comparing themselves with other elderly participants in responding to the question. One elderly person said, "I have no issues with doing things on my own, but I am usual. Look at her, she can do more stuff than I do and she is older than me." Another elderly woman working on her craft project while I went over each question commented: "Other elderly can do much faster than I do." Or they were modestly hesitant to rate their health "very good" since the Japanese culture emphasizes collectivism, not standing out.

When asked about their *ikigai*, the purpose of life, as an open-ended question, the most frequently mentioned phrases were "participating in these activities" (31 respondents) and "talking with their friends" (36 respondents). These counts exceeded the number mentioning their family. Ten of them answered their *ikigai* was to see their kids grow. Several elderly people proudly detailed their children's achievements. The children had left the town for education and a job. The parents looked forward to visiting with their absentee children and grandchildren during holidays or long weekends. When the elderly talked about their children's achievements, there was no expectation of their return to live with the parents in Kawanehonchō, which would downgrade their children's social mobility. Finally, eight of the elderly respondents mentioned growing vegetables to be their *ikigai*. One elderly man in his 70s who needed assistance in filling out the survey was very quiet throughout the survey. When he was asked about his *ikigai*, he became very animated in speaking of his garden and vegetables he grew for his family and friends. Gardening optimizes health not only through better nutrition and physical activity but also through *ikigai*.

When asked the open-ended question of what they thought of the town, three respondents answered that they wanted more interaction with young children. Three elderly people wrote that their town lacked stores; two mentioned the town lacked doctors; and one believed the town lacked recreational facilities. Few cited the inconvenience due to the geographical location. Overall, most elderly emphasized that the town was an inseparable part of their life.

Twenty-six respondents brought up the word "*Sumiyoi*," meaning comfortableness of living. One eldery woman said: "This place is truly *sumiyoi*. I am remaining healthy and want to stay here." Another elderly woman emphasized: "My daughters live in an urban town three hours away, but I want to stay here because I know how to live here." For the elderly, remaining healthy and wishing to stay in the town were almost synonymous. It appeared their strong wish for aging in place committed them to participate in these activities, and these activities also made them hope to age in place. To meet the demand for health care, Kawanehonchō invested in developing a virtual hospital where local doctors can see any tests results the elderly took at hospitals elsewhere and can consult with those non-local physicians. As is the case in rural Japan, "telemedicine" is also being used to provide health care in the rural United States, where doctors and hospitals are scarce (See Grigsby and Goetz 2004). While the majority of the elderly valued the town to be elder-friendly, they were very critical as well. Eight of them wrote that depopulation is a significant problem. Seven of them mentioned the lack of youth as reducing the energy of the town.

Summary

As Kawachi, Kennedy and Glass (1999) suggested, social capital, defined as a public good provided by the community, can positively influence health behaviors through rapid diffusion of health information through lifestyle. These programs increased the likelihood of adopting healthy norms and accepting social control of deviant health-related behaviors. These results suggest the town contains social networks of support, and expectations and willingness to act to maintain a close-knit neighborhood. In other words, the success in these programs is impossible without a high degree of collective efficacy based on mutual trust and support (social cohesion) and expectations and willingness to act for the community (informal social capital). It is impossible without the presence of structural and cognitive dimensions of social capital. The connection between individual and contextual level social capital is so strong that the two levels are almost inseparable. Local people create and participate in programs to support the community, and their efforts provide appreciation and pride on both sides. The payback is not expected, as older ones have supported the young, and to become elderly is on everyone's life course. Such environment motivates many elderly to describe the town as *sumiyoi*.

Several elderly people shared their concern that the town will be merged with the neighboring town in the face of depopulation. In the next chapter, we explore the possibility of inmigration to Kawanehonchō.

~ Nine ~

Elder Migration and the
Future of Rural Japan

There are two major factors that make Kawanehonchō successful at healthy aging without advanced hospitals, advanced degrees, or high-paid jobs. First, the municipal welfare office and the Kawanehonchō Council of Social Welfare (KCSW) office offer locally tailored programs to promote healthy aging by focusing on the prevention of disability and the promotion of social integration. Second, the elderly people, especially those who are free, or relatively free, from physical disability can achieve a healthy life expectancy by relying on cumulative networks of support and the spirit of *otagaisama* that roots them locally. Successful aging in this town suggests that the neighborhood is a distinctive source of structural and cognitive social capital for successful aging. High collective efficacy, consisting of social cohesion and informal social control, leads to longer, greater, and more egalitarian impacts on healthy aging than socioeconomic characteristics. However, a major challenge to the continuation of that success is to avoid further depopulation.

Kawanehonchō is a town created politically in 2005 by merging, for fiscal reasons, two towns that were shrinking due to net outmigration. Several elderly informants in the town voiced apprehension over future mergers of Kawanehonchō with even more adjacent towns. The concern is valid, since there is a nationwide trend of outmigration of youths and young adults from rural to urban Japan in search of education and jobs unavailable at their point of origin. Yet, as we discuss below, the future of economic vitality in rural Japan may depend not only on the outmigration of the young but also on the inmigration of older adults. In this chapter, we discuss what we found during interviews with a small snowball sample of older adults who became inmigrants to the rural area around Kawanehonchō. We conclude the chapter by addressing what it may mean for public policies to stimulate the rural economy of Kawanehonchō and elsewhere in rural Japan.

Rural Inmigration (I-turn) in Japan

In Japan, rural towns increasingly advertise themselves and use brochures to recruit new residents or tourists. Not only Kawahenonchō but also various rural towns in Shizuoka Prefecture created websites that include virtual tours to lure inmigrants, especially people from urban areas. These websites aim to attract newcomers with the promise of healthy lifestyles through locally grown vegetables, clean air, pure water, and breathtaking scenery of natural beauty. According to Tamamura (2007), there was a first 'I-turn' boom around 1980; 'I' in I-turn took the first letter of the word, *inaka,* meaning rural areas. Thus, I-turn refers to people's movement into rural areas. There is no statistical analysis to show how many people have actually moved, but the I-turn around 1980 targeted Baby Boomers, defined in Japan as those born between 1947 and 1949. Entering their 30s, the urban Baby Boomers were made to feel nostalgic by magazines and TV programs featuring natural landscapes (Tamamura 2007). Today, rural areas continue to attract Baby Boomers to settle there after their retirement.

Today's image of I-turn is more diverse, involving more than Baby Boomers. Magazines and TV programs aim to attract people from diverse age groups. There are various books describing people's experience of the I-turn. Some of these I-turners are families in their 20's or 30's, some are families in their 40's moving to rural areas to raise children in nature, and some are single women moving to rural areas to get a new start in their lives (Ijyuu-life kenkyū-kai 2016; Isa 2017). There are books featuring experiences of families with children who hold two houses, one urban and the other one rural, so that they can enjoy the advantages of both environments (Matsuda 1998; Tomoeda 2016). Permaculture, a designing of the environment to be in harmony with the natural ecosystem, became a popular keyword in the media discussing I-turns. Since purchasing agricultural land involves complicated legal paperwork to follow various regulations and requirements, some rural towns started to offer apartments that come with some agricultural land to grow vegetables and rice as well as hands-on assistance from rural residents. Today's improved availability of information technology in rural areas allows people to access goods and information through the internet, and connect with others through social media even if they live in rural areas.

Mitsubishi Research Institute, Inc. conducted a survey in 2013 of 3,567 individuals who were currently living in three metropolitan areas (Tokyo, Nagoya, and Osaka) but hoping to move to rural areas.[1] Table 9.1 summarizes the descriptive statistics of the people who plan to move to rural areas. It shows that 26 percent of people already have a detailed plan. Those in their 40s, 50s, and 60s were more interested in moving to rural areas than others (Figure 9.1). As expected, a majority of those found rich environmental amenities to be a reason for planning to move to rural areas; and almost two-thirds cited air and water quality. The chance to have cheaper and larger residences in rural Japan were seen as a big attraction by urbanites. On the other hand, they saw a lack of transportation and facilities to be possible disadvantages (Table 9.1).

Table 9.1 Descriptive Data Based on People Hoping to Move to Rural Areas

	Frequency (Percentage)
Planning	
Already has a detailed plan	928 (26.0)
Without any detailed plan	2639 (74.0)
When to move	
Less than a year	784 (21.9)
2 to 4 years	1922 (53.8)
More than 4 years	861 (24.1)
Reason for hoping to move to rural areas	
Tired of the noise in urban areas	961 (26.9)
Hoping to move to somewhere more spacious	1086 (30.4)
Hoping to live in area with rich environment and nature	2061 (57.8)

No reason to stay in urban areas after retirement	823 (23.1)
Hoping to change the environment to raise children	435 (12.2)
Hoping to change the work lifestyle	1019 (28.6)
Hoping to find a second home to move back and forth	565 (15.8)
Hoping to go back to where I (or my spouse) grew up	649 (18.2)
Looking for better facilities for the elder care services in the future	253 (7.1)
Hoping/necessity to take care of parents	341 (9.6)
Hoping/necessity to succeed the family business	66 (1.9)

Possible Advantages

Environment (air and water quality)	2296 (64.4)
Housings are more spacious	1257 (35.2)
Cheaper cost of living	1613 (45.2)
Better environment to raise children	492 (13.8)
Have many friends and relatives	496 (13.9)
Have more time to relax and enjoy life	1438 (40.3)
Focus more time on hobbies and recreations	1240 (34.8)
Stronger ties to the neighbors	586 (16.4)
Better healthcare services	174 (4.9)

Possible Disadvantages

Lack of facilities and services such as shopping	1922 (53.9)
Lack of transportation	2065 (57.9)
Lack of healthcare and care services	1420 (39.8)
Lack of cultural facilities such as concert halls and museums	808 (22.7)
Not an ideal environment to raise children	140 (3.9)
Reduced opportunities to see families such as children	390 (10.9)
Reduced income	909 (25.5)
Disturbed by stronger ties to the neighbors	535 (15.0)

Source: Survey on Migration to Rural Areas 2013 conducted by Mitsubishi Research Institute, Inc. The data for this secondary analysis, name of the survey and the name of depositor, were provided by the Social Science Japan Data Archive, Center for Social Research and Data Archives, Institute of Social Science, The University of Tokyo.

While diverse groups of individuals living in metropolitan areas hope to move to rural areas for multiple reasons (Table 9.1), they have access to books that encourage people to stay in urban areas and warn against romantic and nostalgic images of rural areas. Yamazaki (2009) emphasized the advantages of urban living: freedom from the high visibility of rural neighbors,

Figure 9.1 Age of Those Hoping to Move to Rural Areas

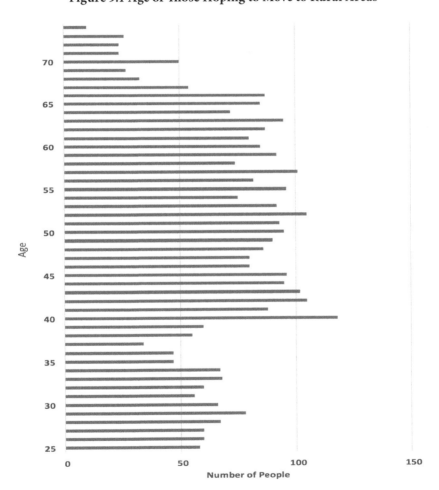

Source: Survey on Migration to Rural Areas 2013 conducted by Mitsubishi Research Institute, Inc. The data for this secondary analysis, name of the survey and the name of depositor, were provided by the Social Science Japan Data Archive, Center for Social Research and Data Archives, Institute of Social Science, The University of Tokyo.

plus the easy access to shopping, hospitals, and theaters. Yamada (2018) described his challenge and hardship of finding a place to live in rural towns for the first time. People would respond to him saying: "There are empty houses, but the owners come back for the summer so they are not available." He noticed that there are various empty houses, but he was told they are unavailable because the owners had left Buddhist altars, boxes, or ancestral graves near the house (Yamada 2018). Yamada talked with a social activist who agreed that it is impossible for outsiders without local connections to find a place to live. Questioning the long-term commitment, some showed reluctance in renting or selling real estate to a newcomer. Similarly, Tamamura (2007) pointed out the difficulty of urban people adjusting to the way rural people communicate. Neighbors commonly leave gifts of vegetables at the doorstep of a house, but this practice could scare off some urbanites.

The first author is from a rural area of Japan, where some close neighbors will enter a house without ringing the doorbell or even if no one answers after calling out their name. Instead of using the entrance, neighbors often enter her parent's house from the back door or the veranda. Borrowing condiments or vegetables, receiving vegetables and snacks, getting advice on medical symptoms from neighbors take place as part of daily life. Her daughters learned origami, coloring, local crafts, language and culture naturally through daily interactions with neighbors. In rural areas, the neighborhood association often consists of adults who have known each other since childhood. The newcomers will automatically join the neighborhood association and each household takes turns in leading activities such as the local sports day and sending volunteers to recycling, funerals, and cleaning up local shrines and community centers. When someone passes away, the neighborhood association sends volunteers to help with the funeral. When someone becomes hospitalized, the neighborhood association collects small amounts of money to deliver as a gift. Her grandmother in her 90s lives alone, but her neighbors frequently visit her to bring vegetables and to chat with her.

Today, rural towns have gradually started to welcome newcomers. Tamamura (2007) points out that people, especially women, are creating hobby groups that bring newcomers into their circle. However, such gradual movement varies from town to town. Recently, the media featured a debate on whether it is a good idea for seniors to move to rural areas where they tend to lack transportation (Kimura 2015). Today's elderly people grew up in a time when there were farms, mountains, and rivers nearby; and many living in urban areas experienced rapid urbanization. They were attracted by the I-turn movement in their 40s and 50s. However, while the data suggest that about 40 percent of those living in Tokyo hope to live in rural areas in the future, it is not easy to make that happen (Yamamoto 1999). Purchasing a house is still considered to be for settling down for good for many Japanese people.

According to another survey conducted by the government for people living in Tokyo, about 51 percent of men in their 50s and 34 percent of women in their 50s hope to move to other regions, and the reasons include going back to where they grew up and hoping to start a slow life (Masuda 2015). In the book describing the experience of rural migration, Yamamoto and his wife explain that their turning point was an earthquake, which they felt was more life-endangering in a city than in a rural place (Yamamoto 1999). In another book, Tawara (2000) describes her fatigue from business with urban life. She finds that even living by herself now in rural Japan keeps her quite busy but unfatigued by pleasurable activities. She describes that her plan for moving to a rural area started in her 40s, and she divorced her husband because he would not move with her to such a place after retirement (Tawara 2000). Obviously, rural areas seem to provide many incentives for older urban adults to move there. However, it is hard to estimate the actual number of people who will act on these desires, since the ability to act not only depends on their successful retirement planning, but also on various other factors including the support from other family members and the readiness of the rural areas to accept newcomers.

Continuing Care Retirement Communities (CCRCs)

The Japanese government and some rural municipal governments had a vision to create Continuing Care Retirement Communities (CCRCs). CCRCs are long-term care options for the elderly people hoping to stay in the same place as they move through different phases of their aging process. CCRCs offer a wide range of services, activities, and care in one place to accomodate the changing needs of the elderly as they age (AARP 2019). Strongly influenced by the idea of the CCRC in the United States, the Japanese government proposed CCRCs in less populated regions for the retiree and his or her family who are relatively healthy. In 2015, about 15 towns were considering to accept a total number of 3,500 elderly newcomers; but it was unclear how many elderly people actually wanted to move to these rural areas and how quickly these towns could develop facilities and services to accept them (Abe 2015).

Retirement migration became visible as early as the 1970s in the United States, and it was also observed in northern Europe and Spain, Italy, Cyprus, and other southern destinations (Brown and Glasgow 2008). Both the U.S. and Europe follow a similar pattern that retirement migration involves mostly internal redistribution rather than international movement (Brown and Glasgow 2008). In the U.S., CCRCs are estimated to have increased from 700 housing more than 100,000 elders in 1986 to 2,100 housing a total of 660,000 by 2005, and it is predicted to increase (Groger and Kinney 2007). In the U.S., CCRC residents are disproportionately represented in the highest income groups, and they tend to be highly educated and in excellent physical and mental health (Groger and Kinney 2007; Sugihara and Evans 2000). Nearly two-thirds charge an entry fee, and the average initial payment is US $329,000, but it can cost one million dollars in some communities. Once they move in, they pay a monthly fee that is between US $2,000 and US $4,000 (AARP 2019). In addition to costs, the spread of CCRCs faces another challenge in the Japanese cultural context. Sending the elderly relative to a distant place could still be a challenge for family members, as they want to avoid the appearance of *ubasute*, a Japanese folktale about heartlessly abandoning old people who can no longer participate in physical labor, especially in rural towns (Masuda 2015). There continues to be a debate on the elderly migration to rural areas as *ubasute*, shifting the burden of care from families to rural communities.

Despite such challenges and the strong will to remain healthy and independent when children are becoming more unreliable for eldercare, CCRCs are emerging in Japan. Matsuda (2017) discussed various possibilities of CCRCs in Japan, such as CCRCs attracting people with local hot springs, advanced hospitals, arts, and amusement parks. A CCRC called "Share Kanazawa," located in Ishikawa Prefecture, is a multigenerational community that includes senior housings, college apartments, a facility for people with disabilities, and the local hot spring that is also available to local residents. In exchange for affordable housing, college students volunteer to maintain the active community (Matsuda 2017, 68–70). "Smart Community Inage" is another good example of a CCRC located in the Inage Ward in Chiba Prefecture, where about 600 active elderly people moved when they were still active and healthy. This community includes facilities such as a gym, music studio, tennis court, and lounge. A couple who moved to this CCRC mentioned that one of the benefits is that shared similar interests with their neighbors leave them unconcerned about what their neighbors think of them (Matsuda 2017, 71–74). Being free from social appearance (*seken* discussed in Chapter 1), it is easier to develop an elderly subculture and friendship through activities, and the CCRCs serve as havens.

The Possibility of a CCRC in Kawanehonchō

As discussed in Chapter 2, Japanese census data suggest a small net inmigration to Kawanehonchō from 2010 to 2015. Overall, the net inmigration to Kawanehonchō between 2010 and 2015 of people aged 60 or older was an excess of 66 inmigrants over outmigrants. Based on the survey we conducted, a majority of the elderly participants in the programs offered through the municipal welfare office and KCSW are those who have lived in the town for all of their lives or after their marriages. The conversations with employees at the municipal office, KCSW, and a non-profit organization that makes pamphlets for tourists and newcomers suggest that these older inmigrants are more likely to be returnees: people who moved out of Kawanehonchō to hold a nonfarm job and then returned after retirement to take care of their parents. If the major reason for returnees is to take care of their elderly parents, the returnees are less likely to join the programs in which their elderly parents participate. Ever increasing numbers of the elderly have already been a challenge for the town, and the town does not appear to hold enough care facilities and staff to provide hands-on care to accommodate great numbers of senior I-turners.

Although the availability of the land suggests the possibility of a CCRC in the future, Kawanehonchō remains a good example of a naturally occurring retirement community (NORC), referring to a community where most senior citizens have aged in place at their homes instead of relocating. However, in the area right outside of Kawanehonchō, there is a community created over time by retirement migration. It is not CCRC nor NORC, but the natural attractions in the area that drew in those who hope to migrate after the retirement, which resulted in creating an unique community.

Who Are the Newcomers?

The area right outside of Kawanehonchō was advertised for sale to new-comers about 20 years ago. Because of the difficulty in locating elderly new-comers in Kawanehonchō, in July and August, 2018, the first author talked with people who had bought land and moved there. A woman in her 80s, who was also our guide, built her house right outside of Kawanehonchō about 20 years ago. She had seen the sale of land advertised in the newspaper. Her parents grew up in the area, and she spent her childhood in Kawanehonchō. Since she and her husband lived in the city right next to Kawanehonchō, they drove there to look at the land and were amazed at the beauty of the landscape and the good quality of the air and water. The lot for sale overlooked a lake. Although she is now a widow, she continues to live in her lake-view home. She holds another house in a nearby city where her eldest son's family lives. She said, "This is where I grew up. Air, food, and water are the best, and I occasionally stop by the local hot spring." She worked full-time before the retirement, and now she occasionally teaches sewing at the community space and displays her sewing works there. Because of her job that required her interpersonal skills, she knows everyone in the neighborhood. She said, "There are 67 houses, and 49 of them are used as summer vacation homes, so 18 homes are occupied by people living there regularly."

Her neighborhood is surrounded by nature, and the turquoise-colored lake is right near the neighborhood. This location is called Ukishima, an artificial lake with a partially submerged mountaintop that looks like a floating island. (Figure 9.2). While walking and driving around the neighborhood, the first author met three retired couples and another widow, who chatted with her. They were extremely kind and friendly, and invited the first author and her guide to their homes for tea. All of them were in their late 60s or in their 70s. They did not grow up in Kawanehonchō, and they had lived in a more populated city when they were young. When the first author explained why she was interviewing, they unanimously emphasized that they fell in love with the nature of this neighborhood, and also agreed with the guide that this area reminds them of their childhoods in a more rural Japan. Prior

Figure 9.2 Scenery Outside of Kawanehonchō

Photo provided by Masako Tatebayashi

to purchasing the land and the house, these newcomers had visited the area as vacationers for long weekends and breaks in order to escape urban pressures by fishing in the lake, camping in the woods, and bathing in the hot springs. All of these retired couples kept their house in the city, and their children live there. Prior to the husband retiring from work, they commuted back and forth and gradually increased the time spent in their home in this rural area. Thus, they are I-turners who lack ancestral roots in the neighborhood.

Each house in the neighborhood of the guide looks unique, as the owners designed them as refuges from the crowded city, busy schedule, and parenting duties. One of the houses looks like a log cabin with a very high ceiling and a beautiful balcony overlooking the lake (Figure 9.3) Another house in the neighborhood has beautiful bird houses. Our guide mentioned that one of her neighbors built the house to resemble the house of her childhood. Although her hometown is far away, the natural surroundings and the house remind her of the town where she grew up.

Our guide and her neighbors built friendships over time, which the first author could observe through their casual conversations over tea about their

Figure 9.3 Balcony Overlooking the Emerald Green Lake

Photo provided by Kimiko Tanaka

walks together through the neighborhood, and their visits to town to attend the theater together. They did not know each other until they purchased the land and built the house, but they built a friendship over time partly due to their shared appreciation of the natural environment and the closeness in their age. Our guide mentioned that at least one person in a household in her neighborhood can drive so that they can go together to the nearest city for shopping, medical check-ups, entertainment, and visiting their children in the city. Thus, their biggest concern appears to be the time when they can no longer drive, and that is possibly the reason they have kept the house in the city. Prior to retirement, they fit the definition of "circular migrants," who shift from one home to another during a year. Although they spend most of their time at their home in this rural area after retirement, their second home in an urban area serves as insurance for the future, especially when they can no longer drive. Despite the high cost of residential properties in Japan, these retired couples can afford to own two homes as the husbands had held pre-retirement jobs that required at least a college degree (e.g., government employees, or managers at large corporations).

Our guide emphasized the cohesive relationships she has had with her neighbors over the decades. She mentioned that she moved to various places since her childhood; thus, it is in her nature that she loves meeting new people. She said it is her best life skill developed through her life course of migration. Many of her neighbors were also accustomed to moving from one city to another for their husbands' jobs prior to the retirement. She finds that neighbors bonded because they share a history of working in the city, moving from one area to another when they were young, and then deciding live in a rural area by attraction to the same area. Thus, migration has been a way of life for these former urbanites, who were not intimidated by the prospect of moving their main home to a rural destination, and they were excited to meet new people and share their stories. Recently our guide and her neighbors created a mutually beneficial non-profit organization so that they can keep their neighborhood clean and safe. She also pointed out that, in addition to the elderly, there is a group of young single people living in the neighborhood who teach paragliding. She hopes more people will move to her neighborhood permanently as it is exciting for her to interact with new people.

Although the neighborhood of urban inmigrants is a short drive from Kawanehonchō, they do not seem to interact closely with people in the town. Although both groups of residents are very welcoming and kind, beneath the surface is a strong group affiliation distinguishing outsiders from insiders. This social boundary is invisible but felt. For instance, local people tend to live on the land they inherited from their ancestors, while urban inmigrants tend to live in houses they designed themselves. Daily gatherings of local elderly people in Kawanehonchō, other than attending programs, tend to be informal and timed spontaneously. They stop by each other's houses without making any appointments, chat about their families and friends, and exchange vegetables. It is a different way of timing social interactions than what is true for urban inmigrants in the neighborhood, who tend to plan group events, such as a meeting where everyone shares pictures of their trips to foreign countries. Other social events in the neighborhood include barbecues and monthly gatherings to cut grass. Planning allows urban migrants to enjoy the solitude away from the busy urban life they had. They enjoy writing emails, chatting by phone and internet with family and friends in cities, working in their own gardens, crafting, painting, traveling, reading, golfing, birdwatching, and shopping in the city.

Differences in the quality of friendship derive from their lifestyle and their life course. Many local elderly in Kawanehonchō who attend programs through the municipal welfare office and KCSW see each other frequently. Many of these elderly people have known each other since childhood or since they moved to the town after marriage. Most of the employees at the municipal welfare office and KCSW are local; thus, they know each other and the elderly people they serve, and they talk in the local dialect as if they are close relatives. The programs are targeted to the local elderly residents, and such a familial environment is crucial, especially for the increasing number of local elderly people living alone in this depopulated town.

Ground golf is a ball sport invented in Japan. It holds somewhat similar rules to traditional golf, but the rules are simpler, easier for anyone to understand, and only requires one club and one ball per player. It does not cost a membership fee or an expensive fee to play ground golf, and it allows players to wear comfortable clothes. It does not require a vast landscape like the traditional golf, and they can set up quickly and play in the local park. Thus, the local elderly in Kawanehonchō love playing ground golf with their neighbors at the local playground. They bring snacks and lunches to enjoy between games, and they enjoy the local tournaments. Casual conversation about when and where to play ground golf next time or who is the best player of ground golf was heard everywhere in Kawanehonchō. By contrast, in a neighborhood right outside of Kawanehonchō, one of the urban I-turners said that her husband was absent because he went out to play "golf," which refers to 18-hole golf at the country club.

Our guide introduced the first author to another couple living in the same neighborhood, who owns two homes: their main residence in Kawanehonchō and a secondary residence in the city. This couple exemplifies how a vacation spot can become so loved that it becomes a retirement residence. The husband once was a high school teacher who visited this area on fieldtrips for his students, and he fell in love with the emerald green lake and the cleanness of the water. Like other retired couples in the neighborhood, he and his wife transitioned to spend more time here as he approached retirement. Now they both consider it home. The same as our guide, they expressed how much they love their neighbors. They have built a log house by purchasing a kit from a company. They said that TV drama staff and actors once used their house for a drama because of the beautiful location. They ran a café together, and the interior of the café is full of their art and antique collections. Owing to their skills in communicating with people not local to this area and because of the

Figure 9.4: Café That Allows Tourists to Enjoy the Beautiful Scenery

Photo provided by Kimiko Tanaka

modern interior and exterior of the café, it became a relaxing location for people, especially from urban areas (Figure 9.4).

In the area right outside of Kawanehonchō, there is an educational, cultural facility that is in a renovated elementary school that had closed due to depopulation (Figure 9.5). It holds classes about the local culture, and it also serves as a unique place for families and friends to stay overnight to enjoy the nature of the area. A French woman in her 20s temporarily lives in the area to study pottery. She works as a staff member at the facility and teaches local children conversational English and French. She came to this area because one of the Japanese pottery artists she admires introduced her to this area. She stays for several months to learn pottery and volunteers to teach languages, and goes back and forth between Japan and France. She is different from others that the first author met in this area not only because of her young age, but also since she lives there temporarily; she borrows the unused old house from local people. Since she lives within walking distance of local people, her local neighbors frequently bring some vegetables and ask if she needs anything. Her friends in France wonder what she does in the middle of

**Figure 9.5: Closed Elementary School Turned into the Facility
to Learn Local Culture**

Photo provided by Kimiko Tanaka

a rural depopulated area of Japan. She tells them that she has so many things, including pottery, that she finds her life to be quite busy. She finds the town to be so beautiful and attractive to foreigners.

She is not the only foreigner attracted to the area. The Shizuoka Shimbun, a major newspaper in Shizuoka Prefecture, recently reported that an American woman with a doctoral degree purchased an old Japanese-style house near Kawanehonchō to renovate it. Her life is going back and forth between this area and Europe for her job at the Food and Agricultural Organization. She emphasized that the natural beauty and the attractiveness of the old Japanese-style houses draw her back repeatedly from Europe (Tsuchiya 2018)."

Signs of Young People's I-turn to Kawanehonchō

Recently, the town published brochures that include the voices of newcomers, who include: a couple who started a bed and breakfast, a woman who started a café, and a man who started farming. The brochure mainly targets people in their 30s, 40s, and 50s by featuring childcare facilities, schools, and employment opportunities thought to encourage movement to the town to raise a family. Based on the interviews that the municipal office conducted of 64 newcomers, nearly 90 percent of them were younger than 50. The website called OZmall features four mothers who moved to Kawanehonchō. One of them worked in Kawanehonchō after she graduated from college because she was interested in farming. She was touched by the warmth of the local people, who helped her to settle down by giving her vegetables. She ended up marrying a local man and now has a child with him; they live with her parents-in-law (OZmall 2015).

The website by Shizuoka Prefectural office that supports migration called "Yutorisuto Shizuoka" featured two people who moved to Kawanehonchō (Shizuoka Prefecture Homepage 2012). One of them worked as a chef in Tokyo, and then moved to Yamanashi Prefecture, then moved to Kawanehonchō because his parents live there. He opened a café for local people and uses local fresh ingredients. He enjoys serving his dishes to local people, and he feels happy to talk with I-turners and support those who have moved to this town through marriage and jobs. The chef believes that it is a big adjustment to move to rural areas like Kawanehonchō and believes that his café helps that adjustment through being a focal point where newcomers and old-timers can meet. Two others featured on the website are both women who moved from Hokkaido (a northern island of Japan) in order to learn more about green tea, and both of them work at Kawanehonchō to support the green tea industry.

At the second floor of the shop that sells local souvenirs and local ready-to-eat side dishes in Kawanehonchō, a married couple with children opened a café. They also moved from an urban area to Kawanehonchō because they fell in love with the mountains. They had never run a café before, but they were assisted by local people to find the right place to open the café and to learn the details of how to run the business. There is also a woman who left the town at age 18 returned to Kawanehonchō to take care of her elderly parents, and opened a green tea café. Lastly, there is a couple moved to the town to practice permaculture, and after 12 years they are offering courses on forest gardens and permaculture (Kawanehonchō Office 2018). These examples show great potentials for Kawanehonchō to revitalize through attracting the young and middle-aged couples to raise children in a beautiful natural setting. At the same time, the below-replacement fertility rate in Japan may signify that couples want to invest in the education of their children, and competitive schools will retain these families in urban areas.

Summary

With the difficulty of locating elderly people who have newly moved to Kawnehonchō, it is plausible to conclude that this increase of inmigration of the elderly are those who migrated back to Kawanehonchō to look after their elderly parents. The town continues to be NORC, not CCRC at this point. Due to depopulation, the town attempts to build stronger bridging social capital through advertising the town to outsiders, however, it is not as successful as Aurora, Nebraska, where they offer newcomers a first-class library, an excellent community center, a hands-on science museum, and the opportunity of taking leadership to revitalize the economy (Flora, Flora, and Gasteyer 2018).

The neighborhood right next to Kawanehonchō was developed for newcomers; thus, the architectural designs are varied. It is unknown whether the newcomers will remain when their health fails or when they can no longer drive. A growth of retirement migration into amenity-rich rural areas might stimulate a demand for local infrastructures to serve the medical and transportation needs of an elderly population. For urban elderly people moving to rural areas, it would greatly matter whether these areas are deliberately promoting inmigration. Kawanehonchō ranks near the top in Shizuoka Prefecture for having the highest proportion of the elderly 65 years old and above (49.5 percent of the population in 2021) (Kawanehonchō Office 2021). The current situation of an ever-increasing number of elderly residents makes it challenging to motivate more elderly people to migrate to Kawanehonchō. Who moves to rural Japan, why they move, and for how long: the longitudinal research on this is still in the early stages, and requires future studies to shed light on these questions.

~ Ten ~

Rural Depopulation and Healthy Aging

The relationship between socioeconomic status (SES) and health has been widely recognized. People of higher SES are associated with better health, lower mortality rates, and higher life expectancy. However, such socioeconomic differences in health appear to vary across nations. For instance, Japanese socioeconomic differences in health and mortality have been historically smaller than the U.S. (Crimmins, Preston, and Cohen 2011). By estimating the probability of survival at age 80 and older in Japan, Sweden, France, England, and the United States for persons born from 1885 and 1889, (Manton and Vaupel 1995, 1232) found that more than in Japan or Europe, the elderly in the U.S. had the best survival rate at age 80 and over; and Japan, the worst. In other words, the selective effect of education on survival was weakest in Japan (than the other nations) prior to age 80 and allowed those who survived to that old age to be more diverse in SES in Japan.

In the U.S., about one in four Americans older than age 65 lives in a small town or other rural area, and this proportion is much higher in some states, such as Maine, where 58 percent of adults older than 65 live in rural areas (Skoufalos et al. 2017, S-3). Compared to the urban and suburban areas, older adults living in rural areas are more disadvantaged in terms of available services, resources, and activities that produce the social "glue" that holds the society together. Geographic isolations and lower SES in rural America are considered as risk factors that contribute to health disparities and lower life expectancy (Skoufalos et al. 2017, S-4). However, our research on Kawanehonchō suggests that not the high degree of education or occupational status, but the high degree of collective efficacy rooted in the feeling of mutual reciprocity creates an environment where elderly people can rely on one another. Our research suggests that the quality of community, not the quantity of advanced hospitals and recreational facilities, brought healthy life expectancy to a depopulated rural town.

Maintaining a high degree of collective efficacy is not easy when the town continues to depopulate. Depopulation could weaken the bonding social capital, threaten networks of reciprocal assistance, and contribute to depression (Knight 2003). However, in Kawanehonchō, our elderly respondents reported a high quality of life, despite the decades of depopulation. The high level of collective efficacy in Kawanehonchō is reflected in no cases of the novel coronavirus in the town until the first case was observed in March 30th, 2021 (The Shizuoka Shimbun 2021a). Still, it is noteworthy that there were only three COVID-19 cases as of June 15th, 2021 in this town since the beginning of the pandemic (Shizuoka Shimbun 2021b).

The elderly are connected with municipal government employees through the phone called "Kawane-phone" the town provides to all households and facilities (Figure 10.1). People living in Kawanehonchō can talk with local people for free using this phone, and about 1,000 phone calls a day are made by local people using it (Kyocera Communication Systems 2016). Not only is the FaceTime feature in this phone used as a way to communicate with one another, but this phone also has a function to show small video clips such as showing school events, healthy daily exercises for the elderly, and a means of medical alerts. For example, it allows municipal employees to check with the elderly through FaceTime. When the first author first talked with the mayor of the town in 2016, the mayor mentioned the importance of virtual communication in a geographically remote, rural town like Kawanehonchō in preparing for an emergency. With some challenges for those who have technical difficulty in fully utilizing the phone and the voices of concerns in regards to the financial burden of phones, the recent pandemic of coronavirus really showed the great potentials of virtual communications in a rural town. The town recently restarted the programs for the elderly with precautions, such as taking temperatures, wearing masks, opening windows, sanitizing everything with alcohol, and making snacks and green tea as take-outs. The programs for caregivers insure that the gathering does not exceed 20 people.

The greater availability of sports gyms, theaters, shopping malls, and multiple modes of public transportation in urban areas can more quickly spread the novel coronavirus. The absence of collective efficacy makes it harder to unite the citizens to a common goal and can prolong the time that the elderly

Figure 10.1 Picture of Kawane-phone

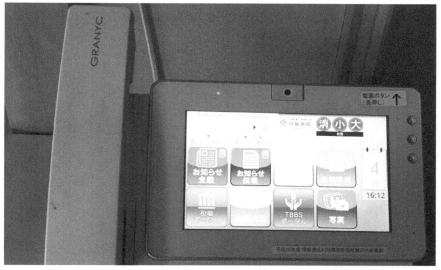

Photo provided by Toshio Tanaka

remain socially secluded due to their fear of seeking outside support. In Klinenberg's (2003) analysis of the mortality due to the Chicago Heat Wave of 1995, he pointed out that so many people died alone, so isolated that their corpses were not discovered for several days. Furthermore, Klinenberg examined two neighborhoods that are next to each other. They have almost identical rates of seniors living in poverty and seniors living alone, but the death rate was much lower in one neighborhood and the physical ecology made the difference between the two: one that was a desolate, high-crime area and one that was a vibrant area where younger residents protected their older, vulnerable residents (Klinenberg 2003). Similarity to the latter neighborhood in Chicago, Kawanehonchō is an excellent example of a small town where the elderly can safely gather because their community members strongly unite for collective safety. Our research shows that the degree of collective efficacy in the community and strong bonding social capital can have great effects on health, possibly greater than the effects of individual socioeconomic status and availability of the advanced facilities and convenient public transportations. "Rural" and "depopulation" should not simply equate with negative outcomes for the elderly.

Some may argue that population density is the major reason why this depopulated rural town kept an extremely low COVID-19 case number since the beginning of the pandemic. However, even with that advantage, the high collective efficacy observed in Kawanehonchō has made neighbors willing to check on the safety of elderly neighbors and the strong bonding social capital has made elderly residents of Kawanehonchō more willing to seek assistance from neighbors.

The threats of acquiring COVID-19 that require social distancing and wearing facial masks may shift the way people think of urban vs. rural areas. There have been reports of older people abandoned in care homes. Ageism is clearly evident through phrases such as #BoomerRemover that emerged in reference to COVID-19. Such ageist prejudices are likely to burden older people with the feeling of worthlessness (Brooke and Jackson 2020). Based on studying 1,310 Spanish people ages 18 to 88 years, the presence of negative stereotypes of aging is one factor associated with the loneliness and psychological distress. The finding suggests that older adults with positive perceptions of aging seem to be more resilient in the time of COVID-19 outbreak (Losada-Baltar et al. 2020). Communities lacking mutual reciprocity may enable people to write or say hurtful things to the elderly population. In such environment, the novel coronavirus may spread quickly.

Recently, some care facilities invited students to interact with the elderly in the United States. Various sources point out that such facilities can reduce age-based prejudice and stereotyping (Burnes et al. 2019; Hagestad and Uhlenberg 2005). Children growing up in a rural town like Kawanehonchō greatly benefited from school programs that invite the elderly population to teach folklore, crafts, cooking, and green tea farming. Rural towns like Kawanehonchō not only benefit children with a clean environment and a smaller classroom size but also with the chances to learn mutual reciprocity across generations.

Revitalizing Rural Towns

One way to solve the economic and social problems from rural depopulation is inmigration of the young and the old. As more Japanese residents of rural towns realize their urgent demographic challenge, with a welcoming heart or reluctance, many rural towns are lowering their boundaries to outsiders. The inmigration of children and their parents is vital to increase fertility rates, keep public schools and facilities for children from closing, and sustain local festivals. Kawanehonchō created an official guidebook for newcomers to advertise the natural beauty, organic products, and availability of high-speed internet. The guidebook emphasizes that, for a family with children, the town offers free healthcare up to high school and small classrooms to give enough attention to each student. For older adults, the guidebook points out that the town is known for healthy aging and great social integration based on mutual reciprocity. It includes the voices of adults moving to the town to achieve their dream of becoming a craftsman, camping ground owner, or farmer (Kawanehonchō Office 2018).

Kawanehonchō and many other rural towns in Japan attempt to attract younger generations with a promise of jobs, such as farming, considered natural and appropriate for rural areas. One major challenge of such campaigns is convincing young, educated people that they can find jobs and cultural niches there. Thus, it is quite important not only to offer job opportunities for merchants and farmers but also for men and women who work in the fields of education, health care, and technology, which require diplomas beyond high school.

Summer tourism has been an important part of the rural economic and population growth in the United States. For example, Lincoln County in Maine has become a year-round residence for people who had previously lived there as summer residents. Sustained seasonal migration has created retirement inmigration and a notable increase in aging-related housing and health services. Obviously, it has created more demands for nurses, physical therapists, and other health professionals (Brown and Glasgow 2008).

Traditionally, Japanese companies offer lifetime employment and seniority-based wages to motivate workers' loyalty, which is then shown by working long hours. Japanese corporate leaders have used the idea of "family" to teach the norm of total commitment: older, parental managers take their subordinates to pubs and restaurants after work to establish a paternalistic social relationship in the informal realm. In a traditional workplace, workers are not only assessed by their ability but also by personality traits beyond one's occupational duties, such as how they contribute to the family-like environment by coming earlier and staying longer than normal hours until their boss leaves the office (Sugimoto 2014, 101–102). Such a traditional work norm reinforces gender inequality, since women with children find it hard to commit to a double-digit and uncertain number of work hours.

As Japan loses population due to declining fertility rates, these traditional Japanese companies must change. Recently, more companies are adopting flex-time at work and telecommuting, allowing workers to work remotely by computer. The current COVID-19 pandemic has increased such trends. A recent survey showed that 70 percent of respondents favor telecommuting (The Japan Times 2020). As more companies offer these options to their employees, it provides greater opportunities for the young, educated people to maintain their work headquartered in a city while enjoying the lifestyle free from pollution and crowds at a rural residence. It will reduce urban traffic that poses serious consequences for the environment. The Japanese government can prevent rural depopulation by assisting urban companies to create rural satellite offices that will allow rural-resident workers to commute shorter distances from home or to telecommute.

Another institutional change crucial to bringing more young people to, or retaining them in, the rural areas is education. Given the shortage of physicians especially in rural areas, the Japanese government rapidly expanded the number of medical school students by adding regional quotas (*chiiki-waku*) since 2008; it accounts for 17 percent of all medical school entrants. These local high school graduates receive a scholarship from the prefectural government in exchange for postgraduate in-prefecture practice (Matsumoto et al. 2016). Many prefectures also have scholarships for non-quota students in exchange for postgraduate in-prefecture practice in rural areas. The obligation term to work is as long as nine years, and notable numbers of young physicians and medical students chose to return their loans instead of fulfilling their duty periods as they consider the obligation term to be too long (Yamamoto et al. 2019, 85). Today, there are also programs for reducing college debts by working in firms in rural districts if college graduates meet certain criteria, including the type of job and length of working at these firms. To encourage more applications, such information should be widely distributed with examples of successful cases to exhibit opportunities that are beneficial, exciting, and promising as it will not benefit anyone if young people are reluctant to move to rural areas.

One of the major limitations is that these economic development programs do not specifically benefit students growing up in rural depopulated areas. Local high schools within rural areas are disadvantaged in placing graduates at high-ranking universities because the highly competitive high schools tend to be located in urban areas. In addition, not treating the depopulated areas separately makes it difficult to benefit students living there. Thus, it is crucial for the government to create scholarships that specifically target students who grow up in depopulated areas defined by the government by the rate of population decrease. For example, scholarships may allow students from depopulated areas to take courses in college on agricultural economics, economic development, or small-business entrepreneurship. These study subjects could benefit rural Japan by reducing regional inequality in education and increasing the diversity in student origins and fields.

Our study suggests that Kawanehonchō holds strong bonding social capital (homogeneous ties), which has been especially helpful in uniting everyone around adherence to public health protocols in the time of the COVID-19 pandemic. In revitalizing the rural towns, building rich bridging social capital to connect the rural community to urban resources is crucial. In Japan, renting an apartment requires the signatures of sponsors. In Kawanehonchō, although the town offers reasonable housing options for couples ages 18-43 with children under age 15, it requires two signatures from residents. This could be quite challenging for those who do not know anyone there. In order to increase the number of couples with children, asking not for local residents' signatures but for anyone credible based on their background check, or changing the rules in case of falling behind on rent payment is necessary. Many of those who are interested in moving into rural towns hope to farm, but it requires lots of skills and complicated paperwork to start farming. Today, some rural towns offer apartments with small areas for them to start farming where local people lecture them how to farm crops. Making housing affordable such as by allowing inmigrants to rent for a trial period before buying could reduce the perceived risks of moving to rural areas.

Recently, there are new coffee shops and restaurants in Kawanehonchō where both locals and newcomers can enjoy beverages and meals. A nonprofit organization offers classes such as badminton, basketball, exercise, and canoeing to their local residents, and supports the gathering of mothers to help one another in raising children. These facilities and programs can build bridging social capital between newcomers and old timers. It is crucial for the national government to invest and support municipal governments in developing greater bridging social capital.

Recommendations for Future Research

As we emphasized in the introduction, words such as "rural" and "depopulation" do not simply imply negative outcomes for the elderly in Japan or the United States. Statistics provide an important overview to understand rural depopulations comparatively from time-to-time and place-to-place. However, to understand successful aging in rural communities, micro-level qualitative studies are crucial.

In our study, without observing programs for the elderly and talking with the local people, we would not have gotten rich information to see how collective efficacy and social capital do matter for their healthy longevity even more than socioeconomic status and the availability of advanced hospitals. For instance, without observing the eldercare programs playing out in Kawanehonchō, we do not know how much the municipal leaders' effort to translate the official documents to the local dialects in a friendly environment greatly matters on the rural elderly's level of engagement and commitment.

Understanding regional variations in-depth would be impossible without building up the relationship of mutual respect and trust between the people facilitating the programs for the elderly and the people of the community. Besides natural attractions in rural Japan, the mutual support of neighbors through friendly conversations and the exchanges of garden products may become a pull factor for the people living in the city. In our future research on Kawanehonchō, we want to study who moved there, who moved back there, and why did they move there. The current study shows that future studies to answer these questions will benefit from multiple qualitative methods used in this book.

Understanding the uniqueness of rural communities allows us to provide great insights to how we can quantitatively measure various aspects of collective efficacy. It would be ideal if more scholars study the elderly in rural depopulated areas through observations, interviews, and the survey not only in Japan but also around the world. Understanding each case located in unique rural localities allows scholars to find themes and patterns with quantitative and qualitative methods beyond the national boundaries. As the elderly continue to change, and the town continues to change due to depopulation and aging, longitudinal studies of depopulated areas will be necessary as well. As Japan continues to experience a decline in population, there may be more foreigners migrating to rural Japanese towns to supplement the labor shortage. In Yamagata prefecture, located in northern Japan, the proportion of foreign spouses has increased over the decades, and the majority of them are women coming from Asian nations including China, the Philippines, and North and South Korea. The high correlation between the proportion of foreign residents and the three generational households suggests that foreign brides are one major factor in maintaining the three generational households in rural farming regions in Yamagata (Kumagai 2014). Rural Japanese towns are quite diverse, often overshadowed by a unified nostalgic traditional image. Understanding the impact of depopulation and aging through case studies is crucial.

Endnotes

Chapter 1

1. Although the line of succession primarily occurred through male primogeniture, there were other forms of succession such as true primogeniture regardless of the sex of the eldest child in some rural areas of Japan until the effects of the Meiji Civil Code became pervasive. At the time of the Meiji Restoration in 1868, male primogeniture was the dominant custom among samurai families, but this was not a legal requirement (Suenari 1972, 122).

2. Premium is income-related. Unless the Category II person is on government support for financial needs, even unemployed people pay for the insurance premiums. For homemakers, their spouse pays for the insurance.

Chapter 2

1. It is called Mutsumi Gakkyū in Japanese.

2. It is called Sukoyaka Daigaku in Japanese.

3. It is called Fuji-no-kuni-gata fukushi service in Japanese.

Chapter 4

1. Care managers are those certified for specialized knowledge in assessing the health levels of the elderly, provide the individual care plan for them, and provide assistance to the elderly in using public services. This role was created in 2000 with the implementation of Japan's long-term care insurance system (LTCI discussed in Chapter 2).

Chapter 5

1. Such a social group is called *ibasho* meaning "the place we belong," discussed in Chapter 2.

2. Kawanehonchō municipal office contacted the office managing the data which allowed us to explore the association between social capital and available health indicators.

Chapter 6

1. *Minsei-iin* refers to welfare commissioners who are commissioned to conduct welfare activities, including consulting and providing advice to people in their regional district in regards to personal problems. These concerns include domestic violence, juvenile delinquency, and social isolation. In appointing this role, the prefectural governor listens to recommendations of the mayor; and the mayor gets recommendations from local citizens. In cities, people consult professionals, such as counselors and psychologists, about personal problems. In rural local communities like Kawanehonchō, it is not rare for people to consult about their personal issues with their district welfare commissioner, and the role is extremely important and well-respected.

Chapter 9

1. The data for this secondary analysis, Survey on Migration to Rural Areas, 2013 (Survey Number 1068) by Mitsubishi Research Institute, Inc., were provided by the Social Science Japan Data Archive, Center for Social Research and Data Archives, Institute of Social Science, The University of Tokyo.

Bibliography

Introduction

Bacsu, Juanita, Bonnie Jeffery, Sylvia Abonyi, Shanthi Johnson, Nuelle Novik, Diane Martz, and Sarah Oosman. 2014. "Healthy Aging in Place: Perceptions of Rural Older Adults." *Educational Gerontology* 40 (5): 327–37. https://doi.org/10.1080/03601277.2013.802191.

Baernholdt, Marianne, Guofen Yan, Ivora Hinton, Karen Rose, and Meghan Mattos. 2012. "Quality of Life in Rural and Urban Adults 65 Years and Older: Findings From the National Health and Nutrition Examination Survey." *Journal of Rural Health* 28 (4): 339–47. https://doi.org/10.1111/j.1748-0361.2011.00403.x.

Blazer, Daniel G., Lawrence R. Landerman, Gerda Fillenbaum, and Ronnie Horner. 1995. "Health Services Access and Use among Older Adults in North Carolina: Urban vs Rural Residents." *American Journal of Public Health* 85 (10): 1384–90. https://doi.org/10.2105/AJPH.85.10.1384.

Brown, David L., and Nina Glasgow. 2008. *Rural Retirement Migration*. New York: Springer.

Burholt, Vanessa, and Christine Dobbs. 2012. "Research on Rural Ageing: Where Have We Got to and Where Are We Going in Europe?" *Journal of Rural Studies* 28 (4): 432–46. https://doi.org/10.1016/j.jrurstud.2012.01.009.

Davis, Sandra, Natalie Crothers, Jeanette Grant, Sari Young, and Karly Smith. 2012. "Being Involved in the Country: Productive Ageing in Different Types of Rural Communities." *Journal of Rural Studies* 28 (4): 338–46. https://doi.org/10.1016/j.jrurstud.2012.01.008.

Elnitsky, Christine, and Betty Alexy. 1998. "Identifying Health Status and Health Risks of Older Rural Residents." *Journal of Community Health Nursing* 15 (2): 61–75.

Grigsby, William, and Stephen J. Goetz. 2004. "Telehealth: What Promises Does It Hold for Rural Areas?" In *Critical Issues in Rural Health*, edited by Nina Glassgow, Lois Wright Morton, and Nan E. Johnson, 237–50. Ames, Iowa: Blackwell Publishing.

Hewitt, Paul S. 2004. "Depopulation and Aging in Europe and Japan." *The Social Contract* 14 (4): 282–87.

Kinsella, Kevin. 2001. "Urban and Rural Dimensions of Global Population Aging: An Overview." *The Journal of Rural Health : Official Journal of the American Rural Health Association and the National Rural Health Care Association* 17 (4): 314–22. http://www.ncbi.nlm.nih.gov/pubmed/12071553.

Kumar, Vinod, Miguel Acanfora, Catherine H. Hennessy, Alex Kalache. 2001. "Health Status of the Rural Elderly." *The Journal of Rural Health : Official Journal of the American Rural Health Association and the National Rural Health Care Association* 17 (4): 328–31. https://doi.org/10.1111/j.1748-0361.2001.tb00282.x.

McLaughlin, Diane K, C Shannon Stokes, and Atsuko Nonoyama. 2001. "Residence and Income Inequality: Effects on Mortality Among U.S. Counties." *Rural Sociology* 66 (4): 579–98. https://doi.org/10.1111/j.1549-0831.2001.tb00085.x.

Matanle, Peter, and Anthony Rausch. 2011. *Japan's Shrinking Regions in the 21st Century: Contemporary Responses to Depopulation and Socioeconomic Decline*. New York: Cambria Press.

Miller, Michael K, C. Shannon Stokes, and William B Clifford. 1987. "Comparison of the Rural-Urban Mortality Differential From Death to From All Causes, Cardiovascular Disease and Cancer." *Rural Health Policy* 3 (2): 23–34. https://doi.org/10.1111/j.1748-0361.1987.tb00165.x.

Norstrand, Julie A., and Qingwen Xu. 2012. "Social Capital and Health Outcomes Among Older Adults in China: The Urban-Rural Dimension." *The Gerontologist* 52 (3): 325–34. https://doi.org/10.1093/geront/gnr072.

Pillemer, Karl, and Nina Glassgow. 2000. "Social Integration and Aging: Background and Trends." In *Social Integration in the Second Half of Life*, edited by Karl Pillemer, Phyllis Moen, Elaine Wethington, and Nina Glasgow, 19–47. Baltimore, MD: John Hopkins University Press.

Satterthwaite, David. 2020. "An urbanising world." International Instituet for Environment and Development, April 9, 2020. https://www.iied.org/urbanising-world.

United Nations. 2014. "World Urbanization Prospects 2014 Revision." July 10, 2014. https://www.un.org/en/development/desa/publications/2014-revision-world-urbanization-prospects.html.

Walsh, Kieran, Eamon O'Shea, Thomas Scharf, and Michael Murray. 2012. "Ageing in Changing Community Contexts: Cross-Border Perspectives from Rural Ireland and Northern Ireland." *Journal of Rural Studies* 28 (4): 347–57. https://doi.org/10.1016/j.jrurstud.2012.01.012.

Ziersch, Anna M., Fran Baum, I. Gusti Ngurah Darmawan, Anne M. Kavanagh, and Rebecca J. Bentley. 2009. "Social Capital and Health in Rural and Urban Communities in South Australia." *Australian and New Zealand Journal of Public Health* 33 (1): 7–16. https://doi.org/10.1111/j.1753-6405.2009.00332.x.

Chapter 1

Abe, Kinya. 1995. *Seken to wa nanika (What Is Seken?)*. Tokyo: Kodan-sha.

Aikawa, Toshihide. 2016. *Kiseki no mura (Rural Community Development in Japan)*. Tokyo: Shueisha.

Akiyama, Naomi, Takeru Shiroiwa, Takashi Fukuda, Sachiyo Murashima, and Kenshi Hayashida. 2018. "Healthcare Costs for the Elderly in Japan: Analysis of Medical Care and Long-Term Care Claim Records." *PLoS ONE* 13 (5): e0190392. https://doi.org/10.1371/journal.pone.0190392.

Aratame, Natsumi. 2007. "Chapter 1 Japan's Community-Oriented Welfare for the Elderly: Its Implications to Asian Developing Countries." In *Aging Population in Asia: Experience of Japan, Thailand and China*, 1–19. Beijing, China: JICA Research Institute. http://open_jicareport.jica.go.jp/pdf/11850484.pdf.

Asai, Masayuki O., and Velma A. Kameoka. 2005. "The Influence of Sekentei on Family Caregiving and Underutilization of Social Services among Japanese Caregivers." *Social Work.* 50 (2): 111–18. https://doi. org/10.1093/sw/50.2.111.

Assmann, Stephanie. 2016. "Introduction." In *Sustainability in Contemporary Rural Japan: Challenges and Opportunities*, edited by Stephanie Assmann, xv–xxv. New York: Routledge.

Atoh, Makoto. 2008. "Family Changes in the Context of Lowest-Low Fertility: The Case of Japan." *International Journal of Japanese Sociology* 17 (1): 14–29. https://doi.org/10.1111/j.1475-6781.2008.00109.x.

Cabinet Office Japan. 2011. "Annual Report on the Aging Society 2011 (White Paper)." Accessed May 25, 2021. https://www8.cao.go.jp/kourei/ whitepaper/index-w.html.

———. 2017. "White Paper on Gender Equality 2017." Accessed May 25, 2021. http://www.gender.go.jp/about_danjo/whitepaper/h29/zentai/ pdf/h29_genjo.pdf.

———. 2020. "A 2020 Declinng Birthrate White Paper." Accessed May 25, 2021. https://www8.cao.go.jp/shoushi/shoushika/whitepaper/ measures/w-2020/r02webhonpen/index.html.

Feldhoff, Thomas. 2013. "Shrinking Communities in Japan: Community Ownership of Assets as a Development Potential for Rural Japan?" *URBAN DESIGN International* 18: 99–109. https://doi.org/10.1057/ udi.2012.26.

Fu, Rong, Haruko Noguchi, Akira Kawamura, Hideto Takahashi, and Nanako Tamiya. 2017. "Spillover Effect of Japanese Long-Term Care Insurance as an Employment Promotion Policy for Family Caregivers." *Journal of Health Economics* 56: 103–12. https://doi.org/10.1016/j. jhealeco.2017.09.011.

Fujinami, Takumi. 2016. *Jinkou-gen ga chihou wo tsuyoku suru (Rrual Towns Strengthened by Depopulation).* Tokyo: Nihon Keizai Shimbun Shuppansha.

Goldstein, Joshua, Tomás Sabotka, and Aiva Jasilioniene. 2009. "The End of the 'Lowest-Low' Fertility?" *Max Planck Institute for Demographic Research Working Paper WP 2009-029.* Accessed May 25, 2021. www. demogr.mpg.de/papers/working/wp-2009-029.pdf.

Hara, Toshihiko. 2015. *A Shrinking Society: Post-Demographic Transition in Japan*. Springer.

Imai, Yukihiko. 1970. *Nihon no kaso chiiki (Depopulated Rural Towns in Japan)*. Tokyo: Iwanami shinsho.

Ishida, Takeshi. 1971. *Japanese Society*. New York: Random House.

Ito, Masami. 2015. "The True Cost of Fertility Treatment in Japan." *Japan Times*, June 20, 2015. https://www.japantimes.co.jp/life/2015/06/20/lifestyle/true-cost-fertility-treatment-japan/.

Kashimura, Aiko. 2013. "Japanese Psychoanalysis as Deciphering the Japanese Unconsciousness and Supporting the Japanese Subject." In *Routledge Companion to Contemporary Japanese Social Theory*, edited by Anthony Eliott, Masataka Katagiri, and Atushi Sawai, 67–89. London and New York: Routledge.

Kitahara, Tetsuya. 1994. "*Kasotaisaku koremade to korekara* (Depopulation Policies Past and Present)." In *Kasochiiki no renaissance*, edited by Toru Hashimoto and Wataru Omori, 35–70. Tokyo: Gyousei.

Kitayama, Shinobu, and Toshie Imada. 2008. "Defending Cultural Self: A Dual-Process Model of Agency." In *Advances in Motivation and Achievement*, edited by Martin L Maehr, Stuart A. Karabenick, and Timothy C. Urdan, 171–207. Emerald Publishing.

Kito, Hiroshi. 2011. *2100nen, jinkou san bun no ichi no nihon (By 2100, Japanese Pouplation Will Be Reduced to One-Third)*. Tokyo, Japan: Media Factory.

Klien, Susanne. 2016. "Young Urban Migrants in the Japanese Countryside between Self-Realization and Slow Life?" In *Sustainability in Contemporary Rural Japan: Challenges and Opportunities*, edited by Stephanie Assmann, 95–107. New York: Routledge.

Knight, John. 2003. "Repopulating the Village?" In *Demographic Change and the Family in Japan's Aging Society*, edited by John W. Traphagan and John Knight, 107–23. New York: State University of New York Press.

Koukami, Shouji. 2006. *Kuuki to seken (Environment and Social Appearances)*. Tokyo: Koudansha Gendai Shinsho.

Kousaka, Ryo. 2012. *Chiiki saisei (Rural Town Rejuvenation)*. Tokyo: Iwanami Shoten.

Kumagai, Fumie. 2008. *Families in Japan: Changes, Continuities, and Regional Variations.* University Press of America.

Livingston, Gretchen. 2019. "Is U.S. Fertility at an All-Time Low? Two of Three Measures Point to Yes." Pew Research Center. May 22, 2019. https://www.pewresearch.org/fact-tank/2019/05/22/u-s-fertility-rate-explained/.

Lützeler, Ralph. 2008. "Regional Demographics." In *The Demographic Challenge: A Handbook about Japan*, edited by Florian Coulmas, Harald Conrad, Annette Schad-Seifert, and Gabriele Vogt, 61–79. Leiden, the Netherlands: Brill.

Matanle, Peter, and A.S Rausch. 2011. *Japan's Shrinking Regions in the 21st Century: Contemporary Responses to Depopulation and Socioeconomic Decline.* New York: Cambria Press.

Matanle, Peter, and Yasuyuki Sato. 2010. "Coming Soon to a City Near You! Learning to Live 'Beyond Growth' in Japan's Shrinking Regions." *Social Science Japan Journal* 13 (2): 187–210. https://doi.org/10.1093/ssjj/jyq013.

Matsubara, Haruo. 1969. "The Family and Japanese Society After World War II." *The Developing Economies* 7 (4): 499–526.

Ministry of Agriculture, Forestry and Fisheries. 2020. "Results from the Census of Agricultural and Forestry." Accessed May 25, 2021. https://www.maff.go.jp/j/tokei/kekka_gaiyou/noucen/2020/index.html.

Ministry of Health, Labour, and Welfare. 2017. "Long-Term Care, Health and Welfare Services for the Elderly." Accessed May 25, 2021. https://www.mhlw.go.jp/english/policy/care-welfare/care-welfare-elderly/.

Ministry of Internal Affairs and Communications. 2015. "*Kasotaisaku no genjou* 2015 (Depopulation Policies Today)." Tokyo, Japan. http://www.soumu.go.jp/main_content/000473003.pdf.

———. 2016. "*Toukei kara mita wagakuni no kōreisha* (Japanese Elderly Based on Statistical Data)." Accessed May 25, 2021. http://www.stat.go.jp/data/topics/pdf/topics97.pdf.

Minorikawa, Osamu, director. 2012. *Jinsei, Irodori (It's a Beautiful Life).* Japan: Showgate. http://www.irodori-movie.jp/.

Miyaguchi, Toshimichi. 2003. *Chiiki wo ikasu (Utilizing Rural Towns).* Tokyo: Taimeido.

Morikawa, Mie. 2014. "Towards Community-Based Integrated Care: Trends and Issues in Japan's Long-Term Care Policy." *International Journal of Integrated Care* 14: e005. https://doi.org/10.5334/ijic.1066.

Narumiya, Chie. 1986. "Opportunities for Girls and Women in Japanese Education." *Comparative Education* 22 (1): 47–52. https://doi.org/10.1080/0305006860220108.

National Institute of Population and Social Security Research. 2014. "Chapter 5. Welfare for the Elderly." In *Social Security in Japan 2014*. Accessed May 25, 2021. http://www.ipss.go.jp/s-info/e/ssj2014/005.html.

———. 2020. "Population Statistics." National Institute of Population and Social Security Research. Accessed May 25, 2021. http://www.ipss.go.jp/syoushika/tohkei/Popular/Popular2020.asp?chap=0.

Nishikawa, Yoshitaka, Masaharu Tsubokura, and Satoru Yamazaki. 2016. "Healthcare Delivery to a Repopulated Village after the Fukushima Nuclear Disaster: A Case of Kawauchi Village, Fukushima, Japan." *Japan Medical Association Journal* 59(4): 159–61.

Noda, Kimio. 2012. *Rekishi to shakai no.5: Nihon nougyou no hatten ronri (History and Society 5)*. Tokyo, Japan: Nousan Gyoson Bunka Kyōkai.

Odagiri, Tokumi. 2014. *Nousanson Saisei (Rural Towns Rejuvenation)*. Tokyo, Japan: Iwanami.

OECD. 2013. "Highlights from A Good Life in Old Age? Monitoring and Improving Quality in Long-Term Care." Accessed May 25, 2021. https://www.oecd.org/els/health-systems/Japan-OECD-EC-Good-Time-in-Old-Age.pdf.

Onishi, Takashi. 2011. "*Kokudo keikaku no shiten kara mita shūraku mondai* (Understanding Social Issues Regarding Local Communities through the Viewpoint of the Land Development)." In *Shūraku saisei (Developing Local Communities)*, edited by Takashi Onishi, Tokumi Odagiri, Ryohei Nakamura, Hiroki Yasujima, and Kou Fujiyama, 1–34. Tokyo: Gyousei.

Palmer, Edwina. 1988. "Planned Relocation of Severely Depopulated Rural Settlements: A Case Study from Japan." *Journal of Rural Studies*. 4(1): 21–34. https://doi.org/10.1016/0743-0167(88)90076-9.

Rausch, Anthony S. 2016. "The Heisei Municipal Mergers." In *Sustainability in Contemporary Rural Japan: Challenges and Opportunities*, edited by Stephanie Assmann, 35–48. Routledge.

Raymo, James M. 2003. "Premarital Living Arrangements and the Transition to First Marriage in Japan." *Journal of Marriage and Family* 65 (2): 302–15. https://doi.org/10.1111/j.1741-3737.2003.00302.x.

Ricart, Ender. 2014. "America's Aging Society Problem: A Look to Japan for Lessons on Prevention." *Asia Pacific Bulletin* 282. https://www.eastwest-center.org/publications/americas-aging-society-problem-look-japan-lessons-prevention.

Sakane, Yoshihiko. 2011. *Ie to mura: Nihon dentou shakai to keizai hatten (Japanese Traditional Society and the Economic Development in Pre-War Japan)*. Tokyo, Japan: Rural Culture Association Japan.

Shimada, Chiho, Ryo Hirayama, Tomoko Wakui, Kazuhiro Nakazato, Shuichi Obuchi, Tatsuro Ishizaki, and Ryutaro Takahashi. 2016. "Reconsidering Long-Term Care in the End-of-Life Context in Japan." *Geriatrics Gerontology International* 16 (1): 132–39. https://doi.org/10.1111/ggi.12736."

Statistic Bureau of Japan. 2019. "Statistical Handbook of Japan 2019." Accessed on May 25, 2021. https://www.stat.go.jp/english/data/handbook/pdf/2019all.pdf.

Su, Guandong, Hidenori Okanishi, and Lin Chen. 2018. "Spatial Pattern of Farmland Abandonment in Japan: Identification and Determinantso Title." *Sustainability* 10, 3676. https://doi.org/10.3390/su10103676.

Suenari, Michio. 1972. "First Child Inheritance in Japan." *Ethnology*. 11(2): 122–26. https://doi.org/10.2307/3773295.

Sugimoto, Yoshio. 2014. *An Introduction to Japanese Society*. Cambridge University Press.

Takano, Kazuyoshi. 2009. "*Chiiki no koureika to fukushi.*" (Regional aging and Social Welfare") In *Chihou kara no shakaigaku (Regional Sociology)*, edited by Masae Tsutsumi, Sadao Tokuno, and Tsutomu Yamamoto, 118–39. Tokyo, Japan.

Takegawa, Toshio. 2012. "*Jyūmin sanka de tsukuru jizoku kanou na chiiki fukushi system* (Developing Regional Social Support System That Involves Participation of Local People)." In *Kasochiiki no senryaku (Strategies for Depopulated Areas)*, edited by Keishi Tanimoto and Yoshihiko Hosoi, 90–100. Kyoto.

Tama, Shinnosuke. 2014. "Changes in the Number of Farm Households and Its Regional Character from 1908–1940 in Japan." *Journal of Rural*

Economics 86 (1): 1–11. https://ageconsearch.umn.edu/bitstream/ 242330/2/Tama-14.pdf.

Tan, Zheng. 2006. "Migration of Rural Over Population and Formation of Urban Labor Force in Modern Japan." *The Journal of the Study of Modern Society and Culture* 36: 157–72. http://dspace.lib.niigata-u.ac.jp/ dspace/bitstream/10191/6355/1/01_0009.pdf.

Tanaka, Kimiko, and Miho Iwasawa. 2010. "Aging in Rural Japan—Limitations in the Current Social Care Policy." *Journal of Aging & Social Policy* 22 (4): 394–406. doi: 10.1080/08959420.2010.507651.

Tanaka, Kimiko, and Nan E. Johnson. 2008. "The Shifting Roles of Women in Intergenerational Mutual Caregiving in Japan: The Importance of Peace, Population Growth, and Economic Expansion." *Journal of Family History* 33 (1): 96–120. https://doi.org/10.1177/036319900 7308600.

Tanimoto, Keishi. 2012. "*Kaso chiiki no kongo to kadaikaiketsu no senryaku* (Depopulation Trends and Strategies for Depopulated Areas)." In *Kasochiiki no senryaku (Strategies for Depouplated Areas)*, edited by Keishi Tanimoto and Yoshihiko Hosoi, 12–23. Kyoto: Gakugei Shuppansha.

Thompson, Christopher S. 2008. "Population Decline, Municipal Amalgamation, and the Politics of Folk Performance Preservation in Northeast Japan." In *The Demographic Challenge: A Handbook about Japan*, edited by Florian Coulmas, Harald Conrad, Annette Schad-Seifert, and Gabriele Vogt, 361–86. Brill.

Traphagan, John W. 2004. *The Practice of Concern: Ritual, Well-Being, and Aging in Rural Japan*. Durham, NC: Carolina Academic Press.

Traphagan, John W, and Christopher S. Thompson. 2006. "The Practice of Tradition and Modernity in Contemporary Japan." In *Wearing Cultural Styles in Japan*, edited by John W Traphagan and Christopher S Thompson, 2–24. New York: SUNY Press.

Tsutsumi, Kenji. 2011. *Jinkō genshō kōreika to seikatsu kankyo. (The effect of depopulation on the environment for the elderly.)* Fukuoka: Kyushu Shuppan.

Ueno, Chizuko. 2013. "Family Stategy on Care: Norms, Preferences, and Resources." *Japanese Journal of Family Sociology* 25 (1): 30–42. https:// www.jstage.jst.go.jp/article/jjoffamilysociology/25/1/25_30/_pdf.

United Nations. 2015. "Government Response to Low Fertility in Japan." Accessed May 25, 2021. https://www.un.org/en/development/desa/population/events/pdf/expert/24/Policy_Briefs/PB_Japan.pdf.

United Nations Development Programme. 2019. *Inequalities in Human Development in the 21st Century (Briefing note for countries on the 2019 Human Development Report – Japan).* New York: United Nations Development Programme.

te Velde, Egbert, Dik Habbema, Henri Leridon, and Marinus Eijkemans. 2012. "The Effect of Postponement of First Motherhood on Permanent Involuntary Childlessness and Total Fertility Rate in Six European Countries since the 1970s." *Human Reproduction* 27(4): 1179–83. https://doi.org/10.1093/humrep/der455.

Wakui, Tomoko, Tami Saito, Emily M. Agree, and Ichiro Kai. 2012. "Effects of Home, Outside Leisure, Social, and Peer Activity on Psychological Health among Japanese Family Caregivers." *Aging & Mental Health* 16 (4): 500–6. https://doi.org/10.1080/13607863.2011.644263.

Yamashita, Yusuke. 2015. *Genkai shūraku no shinjitsu.* (The reality of marginal communities.) Tokyo, Japan: Chikuma Shinsho.

Chapter 2

Brown, David L., and Nina Glasgow. 2008. *Rural Retirement Migration.* New York: Springer.

Elizalde-San Miguel, Begoña, and Vicente Díaz-Gandasegui. 2016. "Aging in Rural Areas of Spain: The Influence of Demography on Care Strategies." *History of the Family* 21(2): 214–30. https://doi.org/10.1080/10816 02X.2016.1157828.

Fukase, Kozo. 2008. "Production and Marketing of the High-Quality Tea in Kawane Area, Shizuoka Prefecture." *Geographical Space* 1 (2): 142–59. https://ci.nii.ac.jp/naid/130006699465/en.

Kaneko, Shoji. 2009. "An Examination of Social Participation in Community Business in the Depopulated Regions That Suffer Heavy Snowfall." *Kyoei Gakuen Junior College Departmental Bulletin Paper* 25: 177–96. https://core.ac.uk/download/pdf/228686724.pdf.

Kato, Akihiko. 2013. "The Japanese Family System: Change, Continuity, and Regionality over the Twentieth Century." *MPIDR Working Paper WP 2013-004.* https://www.demogr.mpg.de/papers/working/wp-2013-004.pdf.

Kawanehonchō Office. 2008. "Kawanehonchō Newsletter." *Kawanehonchō Newsletter* no. 37. http://www.town.kawanehon.shizuoka.jp/material/files/group/5/83006715.pdf.

———. 2018. "Statistics of Kawanehonchō." Kawanehonchō Municipal Government Website. Accessed May 25, 2021. http://www.town.kawanehon.shizuoka.jp/material/files/group/1/h30-toukeiyouran.pdf.

Konuma, Minori. 2019. "*Yume no Tsuribashi* (The Dream Supension Bridge)." The Shizuoka Shimbun and Shizuoka Broadcasting Sytem, November 8, 2019. http://www.at-s.com/blogs/minori/2019/11/post_2131.html.

Matsumoto, Kaori. 2009. "*Utsuroi yuku utauta* (Changing Folk Songs in Kawanehonchō)." Shizuoka, Japan. https://shizuoka.repo.nii.ac.jp/?action=pages_view_main&active_action=repository_view_main_item_detail&item_id=3923&item_no=1&page_id=13&block_id=21.

Morikawa, Mie. 2014. "Towards Community-Based Integrated Care: Trends and Issues in Japan's Long-Term Care Policy." *International Journal of Integrated Care* 14: e005. https://doi.org/10.5334/ijic.1066.

National Statistics Center. n.d. "E-Stat (Portal Site of Offical Statistics of Japan)." Accessed May 25, 2021. https://www.e-stat.go.jp/en.

Shahar, Suzana, Jane Earland, and S. Abd Rahman. 2001. "Social and Health Profiles of Rural Elderly Malays." *Singapore Medical Journal* 42 (5): 208–13.

Shizuoka Prefecture Homepage. 2017. "*Otasshado* (Healthy Life Expectancy in Shizuoka)." Accessed May 25, 2021. https://www.pref.shizuoka.jp/kousei/ko-430/kenzou/kenkoujyumyou/otassha29.html.

———. 2020. "Top Level Healthy Life Expectancy in Shizuoka Prefecture." Accessed May 25, 2021. http://www.pref.shizuoka.jp/kousei/ko-430/kenzou/kenkoujyumyou.html.

Shyrock, Henry S, and Jacob S Siegel. 1976. *The Methods and Materials of Demography.* New York: Academic Press, condensed edition by Edward Stockwell.

Symens, Amy, and Edward Trevelyan. 2019. "The Older Population in Rural America: 2012-2016." *American Community Survey Reports.* https://www.census.gov/content/dam/Census/library/publications/2019/acs/acs-41.pdf.

Chapter 3

Ahern, Jennifer, and Sandro Galea. 2011. "Collective Efficacy and Major Depression in Urban Neighborhoods." *American Journal of Epidemiology.* 173 (12): 1453–62. https://doi.org/10.1093/aje/kwr030.

Aida, Jun, Tomoya Hanibuchi, Miyo Nakade, Hiroshi Hirai, Ken Osaka, and Katsunori Kondo. 2009. "The Different Effects of Vertical Social Capital and Horizontal Social Capital on Dental Status: A Multilevel Analysis." *Social Science and Medicine* 69 (4): 512–18. https://doi.org/10.1016/j.socscimed.2009.06.003.

Aida, Jun, Katsunori Kondo, Naoki Kondo, Richard G Watt, Aubrey Sheiham, and Georgios Tsakos. 2011. "Income Inequality, Social Capital and Self-Rated Health and Dental Status in Older Japanese." *Social Science & Medicine* 73 (10): 1561–68. https://doi.org/10.1016/j.socscimed.2011.09.005.

Airey, Laura. 2003. "'Nae as Nice a Scheme as It Used to Be': Lay Accounts of Neighbourhood Incivilities and Well-Being." In *Health and Place* 9: 129–37. https://doi.org/10.1016/S1353-8292(03)00013-3.

Ansari, Sami. 2013. "Social Capital and Collective Efficacy: Resource and Operating Tools of Community Social Control." *Journal of Theoretical and Philosophical Criminology* 5 (2): 75–94.

Baum, Fran E, and Anna M Ziersch. 2003. "Social Capital." *Journal of Epidemiology and Community Health* 57 (5): 320–23. https://doi.org/10.1136/jech.57.5.320.

Berkman, Lisa F, Thomas A Glass, Ian Brissette, and Teresa Seeman. 2000. "From Social Integration to Health: Durkheim in the New Millennium." *Social Science & Medicine* 51 (6): 843–57. https://doi.org/10.1016/S0277-9536(00)00065-4.

Berkman, Nancy D, Stacey L Sheridan, Katrina E Donahue, David J
Halpern, and Karen Crotty. 2011. "Low Health Literacy and Health
Outcomes: An Updated Systematic Review." *Annals of Internal Medicine.* 155(2): 97–107. https://doi.org/10.7326/0003-4819-155-2-
201107190-00005.

Bourdieu, Pierre. 1986. "The Forms of Capital." In *Handboot of Theory and
Research for the Sociology of Education,* edited by John D. Richardson,
241–58. New York: Greenwood Press.

Brown, David L., and Nina Glasgow. 2008. *Rural Retirement Migration.*
New York: Springer.

Cagney, Kathleen A., Thomas A. Glass, Kimberly A. Skarupski, Lisa L.
Barnes, Brian S. Schwartz, and Carlos F. Mendes De Leon. 2009.
"Neighborhood-Level Cohesion and Disorder: Measurement and
Validation in Two Older Adult Urban Populations." *Journals of Geron-
tology - Series B Psychological Sciences and Social Sciences* 64 (3):
415–24. https://doi.org/10.1093/geronb/gbn041.

Cannuscio, Carolyn, Jason Block, and Ichiro Kawachi. 2003. "Social Capital
and Successful Aging: The Role of Senior Housing." In *Annals of
Internal Medicine* 139: 395–99. https://doi.org /10.7326/
0003-4819-139-5_Part_2-200309021-00003.

Cohen, Deborah A., Thomas A. Farley, and Karen Mason. 2003. "Why Is
Poverty Unhealthy? Social and Physical Mediators." *Social Science and
Medicine* 57 (9): 1631–41. https://doi.org/10.1016/
S0277-9536(03)00015-7.

Cohen, Deborah A., Brian K. Finch, Aimee Bower, and Narayan Sastry.
2006. "Collective Efficacy and Obesity: The Potential Influence of
Social Factors on Health." In *Social Science and Medicine,* 62: 769–78.
https://doi.org/10.1016/j.socscimed.2005.06.033.

Cramm, Jane M., Hanna M. Van Dijk, and Anna P. Nieboer. 2013. "The
Importance of Neighborhood Social Cohesion and Social Capital for
the Well Being of Older Adults in the Community." *Gerontologist* 53 (1):
142–50. https://doi.org/10.1093/geront/gns052.

Cummins, Steven, Sarah Curtis, Ana V. Diez-Roux, and Sally Macintyre. 2007. "Understanding and Representing 'place' in Health Research: A Relational Approach." *Social Science and Medicine* 65 (9): 1825–38. https://doi.org/10.1016/j.socscimed.2007.05.036.

Drakulich, Kevin M. 2014. "Social Capital and Collective Efficacy." In *Encyclopedia of Criminology and Criminal Justice*, edited by Gerben Bruinsma and David Weisburd. New York, NY: Springer. https://link.springer.com/referenceworkentry/10.1007%2F978-1-4614-5690-2_428.

Durkheim, Émile. 1984. *The Division of Labor in Society*. New York: Free Press.

Durkheim, Émile, Steven Lukes, and H.D. Halls. 1982. *The Rules of Sociological Method*. New York: The Free Press.

Engström, Karin, Fredrik Mattsson, Anders Järleborg, and Johan Hallqvist. 2008. "Contextual Social Capital as a Risk Factor for Poor Self-Rated Health: A Multilevel Analysis." *Social Science and Medicine* 66 (11): 2268–80. https://doi.org/10.1016/j.socscimed.2008.01.019.

Flora, Corneria Butler, and Jan L. Flora. 2012. *Rural Communities*. Westview Press.

Flora, Corneria Butler, Jan L. Flora, and Stephen P. Gasteyer. 2018. *Rural Communities*. 4th ed. Routledge.

Galinsky, Adena M., Kathleen A. Cagney, and Christopher R. Browning. 2012. "Is Collective Efficacy Age Graded? The Development and Evaluation of a New Measure of Collective Efficacy for Older Adults." *Journal of Aging Research* 2012. https://doi.org/10.1155/2012/360254.

Gofman, Alexander. 2019. "Tradition, Morality and Solidarity in Durkheim's Theory." *İstanbul Üniversitesi Sosyoloji Dergisi*. 39(1): 25–39. https://doi.org/10.26650/sj.2019.39.1.0007.

Hamano, Tsuyoshi, Yoshikazu Fujisawa, Yu Ishida, S. V. Subramanian, Ichiro Kawachi, and Kuninori Shiwaku. 2010. "Social Capital and Mental Health in Japan: A Multilevel Analysis." *PLoS ONE* 5 (10). https://doi.org/10.1371/journal.pone.0013214.

Hanibuchi, Tomoya, Yohei Murata, Yukinobu Ichida, Hiroshi Hirai, Ichiro Kawachi, and Katsunori Kondo. 2012. "Place-Specific Constructs of Social Capital and Their Possible Associations to Health: A Japanese

Case Study." *Social Science and Medicine* 75 (1): 225–32. https://doi. org/10.1016/j.socscimed.2012.03.017.

Hibino, Yuri, Jiro Takaki, Keiki Ogino, Yasuhiro Kambayashi, Yoshiaki Hitomi, Aki Shibata, and Hiroyuki Nakamura. 2012. "The Relationship between Social Capital and Self-Rated Health in a Japanese Population: A Multilevel Analysis." *Environmental Health and Preventive Medicine.* 17(1): 44–52. https://doi.org/10.1007/s12199-011-0218-x.

Hickey, Kathleen T, Ruth M Masterson Creber, Meghan Reading, Robert R Sciacca, Teresa C Riga, Ashton P Frulla, and Jesus M Casida. 2018. "Low Health Literacy: Implications for Managing Cardiac Patients in Practice." *Nurse Practitioner* 43 (8): 49–55. doi: 10.1097/01.NPR.0000 541468.54290.49.

Ichida, Yukinobu, Katsunori Kondo, Hiroshi Hirai, Tomoya Hanibuchi, Goshu Yoshikawa, and Chiyoe Murata. 2009. "Social Capital, Income Inequality and Self-Rated Health in Chita Peninsula, Japan: A Multi-level Analysis of Older People in 25 Communities." *Social Science and Medicine* 69 (4): 489–99. https://doi.org/10.1016/j.socscimed.2009.05. 006.

Kawachi, Ichiro, Bruce P. Kennedy, and Roberta Glass. 1999. "Social Capital and Self-Rated Health: A Contextual Analysis." *American Journal of Public Health* 89 (8): 1187–93. https://doi.org/10.2105/ AJPH.89.8.1187.

Kushner, Howard I., and Claire E. Sterk. 2005. "The Limits of Social Capital: Durkheim, Suicide, and Social Cohesion." *American Journal of Public Health* 95 (7): 1139–43. https://doi.org/10.2105/AJPH.2004. 053314.

Li, Qiuju, Xudong Zhou, Minmin Jiang, and Lu Li. 2017. "The Effect of Migration on Social Capital and Depression among Older Adults in China." *Social Psychiatry and Psychiatric Epidemiology* 52 (12): 1513–22. doi: 10.1007/s00127-017-1439-0.

Mansyur, Carol, Benjamin C. Amick, Ronald B. Harrist, and Luisa Franzini. 2008. "Social Capital, Income Inequality, and Self-Rated Health in 45 Countries." *Social Science and Medicine* 66 (1): 43–56. https://doi. org/10.1016/j.socscimed.2007.08.015.

Matsaganis, Matthew D., and Holley A. Wilkin. 2015. "Communicative Social Capital and Collective Efficacy as Determinants of Access to

Health-Enhancing Resources in Residential Communities." *Journal of Health Communication* 20 (4): 377–86. https://doi.org/10.1080/10810730 .2014.927037.

Meijer, Marlies, and Josefina Syssner. 2017. "Getting Ahead in Depopulating Areas - How Linking Social Capital Is Used for Informal Planning Practices in Sweden and The Netherlands." *Journal of Rural Studies* 55: 59–70. https://doi.org/10.1016/j.jrurstud.2017.07.014.

Meng, Tianguang, and He Chen. 2014. "A Multilevel Analysis of Social Capital and Self-Rated Health: Evidence from China." *Health & Place* 27: 38–44. https://doi.org/10.1016/j.healthplace.2014.01.009.

Mohan, John, Liz Twigg, Steve Barnard, and Kelvyn Jones. 2005. "Social Capital, Geography and Health: A Small-Area Analysis for England." *Social Science and Medicine* 60 (6): 1267–83. https://doi.org/10.1016/j. socscimed.2004.06.050.

Mohnen, Sigrid M., Sven Schneider, and Mariël Droomers. 2019. "Neighborhood Characteristics as Determinants of Healthcare Utilization- A Theoretical Model." *Health Economics Review* 9(1): 7. https://doi. org/10.1186/s13561-019-0226-x.

Moore, Spencer, Mark Daniel, Lise Gauvin, and Laurette Dubé. 2009. "Not All Social Capital Is Good Capital." *Health and Place* 15 (4): 1071–77. https://doi.org/10.1016/j.healthplace.2009.05.005.

Murayama, Hiroshi, Tomoko Wakui, Reiko Arami, Ikuko Sugawara, and Satoru Yoshie. 2012. "Contextual Effect of Different Components of Social Capital on Health in a Suburban City of the Greater Tokyo Area: A Multilevel Analysis." *Social Science and Medicine* 75 (12): 2472–80. https://doi.org/10.1016/j.socscimed.2012.09.027.

Pillemer, Karl, and Nina Glasgow. 2000. "Social Integration and Aging: Background and Trends." In *Social Integration in the Second Half of Life*, edited by Karl Pillemer, Phyllis Moen, Elaine Wethington, and Nina Glasgow, 19–47. Baltimore, MD: John Hopkins University Press.

Poortinga, Wouter. 2006. "Social Relations or Social Capital? Individual and Community Health Effects of Bonding Social Capital." *Social Science & Medicine* 63: 255–70. https://doi.org/10.1016/j. socscimed.2005.11.039.

Portes, Alejandro. 2009. "Social Capital: Its Origins and Applications in Modern Sociology." *Annual Review of Sociology* 24: 1–24. https://doi.org/10.1146/annurev.soc.24.1.1.

Quatrin, Louise Bertoldo, Rosangela Galli, Emilio Hideyuki Moriguchi, F??bio Leite Gastal, and Marcos Pascoal Pattussi. 2014. "Collective Efficacy and Depressive Symptoms in Brazilian Elderly." *Archives of Gerontology and Geriatrics* 59 (3): 624–29. https://doi.org/10.1016/j.archger.2014.08.001.

Rojas, Yerko, and Per Carlson. 2006. "The Stratification of Social Capital and Its Consequences for Self-Rated Health in Taganrog, Russia." *Social Science and Medicine* 62 (11): 2732–41. https://doi.org/10.1016/j.socscimed.2005.11.007.

Sampson, Robert J, Stephen W Raudenbush, and Felton Earls. 1997. "Neighborhoods and Violent Crime: A Multilevel Study of Collective Efficacy." *Science* 277 (5328): 918–24. https://doi.org/10.1126/science.277.5328.918.

Skrabski, Árpád. 2003. "Social Capital in a Changing Society: Cross Sectional Associations with Middle Aged Female and Male Mortality Rates." *Journal of Epidemiology & Community Health* 57 (2): 114–19. https://doi.org/10.1136/jech.57.2.114.

Skrabski, Árpád, Maria Kopp, and Ichiro Kawachi. 2004. "Social Capital and Collective Efficacy in Hungary: Cross Sectional Associations with Middle Aged Female and Male Mortality Rates." *Journal of Epidemiology and Community Health* 58 (4): 340–45. https://doi.org/10.1136/jech.2003.010017.

Snelgrove, John W, Hynek Pikhart, and Mai Stafford. 2009. "A Multilevel Analysis of Social Capital and Self-Rated Health: Evidence from the British Household Panel Survey." *Social Science & Medicine* 68 (11): 1993–2001. https://doi.org/10.1016/j.socscimed.2009.03.011.

Thompson, Estina E, and Neal Krause. 1998. "Living Alone and Neighborhood Characteristics as Predictors of Social Support in Late Life." *Journals of Gerontology Series B: Psychological Sciences & Social Sciences* 53B (6): S354–S364. https://doi.org/10.1093/geronb/53B.6.S354.

Verhaeghe, Pieter-Paul, and Gindo Tampubolon. 2012. "Individual Social Capital, Neighbourhood Deprivation, and Self-Rated Health in England." *Social Science & Medicine (1982)* 75 (2): 349–57. https://doi.org/10.1016/j.socscimed.2012.02.057.

Webb, Stephen D. 1972. "Crime and the Division of Labor: Testing a Durkheimian Model." *American Journal of Sociology* 78 (3): 643–56. https://doi.org/10.1086/225368.

Whitley, Rob. 2008. "Social Capital and Public Health. Qualitative and Ethnographic Approaches." In *Social Capital and Health*, edited by Ichiro Kawachi and S.V. Subramanian, 95–115. New York: Springer.

Yen, Irene H., Yvonne L. Michael, and Leslie Perdue. 2009. "Neighborhood Environment in Studies of Health of Older Adults. A Systematic Review." *American Journal of Preventive Medicine* 37(5): 455–63. https://doi.org/10.1016/j.amepre.2009.06.022.

Chapter 4

Cabinet Office Japan. 2006. "*Shōshika taisaku to kazoku, chiiki no kizuna ni kansuru isiki chōsa* (Survey on the Perception towards Regional Social Integration)." Accessed May 25, 2021. https://www8.cao.go.jp/shoushi/shoushika/research/cyousa18/kizuna/html/1mokuji.html.

———. 2013. "*Kōreisha no chiiki shakai e no sanka ni kansuru ishiki chōsa* (Survey of the Elderly on Their Participation in Their Society/Community)." Accessed May 25, 2021. https://www8.cao.go.jp/kourei/ishiki/h25/sougou/zentai/index.html.

City of Yokohama. 2013. "*Kōnan kumin ishiki chōsa* (Survey on Kōnan Ward)." Accessed May 25, 2021. https://www.city.yokohama.lg.jp/konan/kusei/tokei/past_ishiki.html.

Kagawa Prefectural Government. 2012. "*Kōreisha ibasho jittai chōsa* (The Survey on the *ibasho* of the elderly")." Takamatsu, Japan: Kagawa Prefectural Government Health and Welfare Department.

Shizuokaken Sōgō Kenkō Center. 2016. *Kōreisha seikatsu jittai chōsa (Survey to Understand the Lifestyles of the Elderly)*. Shizuoka City: Shizuokaken Sōgō Kenkō Center.

Chapter 5

Kawanehonchō. 2015. 7th *Kawanehonchō kōreisha hoken fukushi keikaku &*
6th Kawanehonchō kaigohoken jigyou keikaku (Municipal Social Welfare
Plan in Kawanehoncho for the Elderly). Kawanehonchō office.

Kawanehonchō Council of Social Welfare. 2015. *2nd Kawanehonchō chiiki*
fukushi katsudou keikaku (2nd Plan for the Regional Support for the
Elderly). Kawanehonchō. Kawanehonchō Council of Social Welfare.

Oguni, Itaro. 2000. "*Ryokucha no kinousei* (Benefits of Green Tea)." *Shi-*
zuoka Kenritu Daigaku Tanki Daigakubu Kenkyū Kiyou 14 (1): 77–88.
https://dl.ndl.go.jp/info:ndljp/pid/8799982.

Shizuokaken Sōgō Kenkō Center. 2016. *Kōreisha seikatsu jittai chōsa*
(Survey to Understand the Lifestyles of the Elderly). Shizuoka City:
Shizuokaken Sōgō Kenkō Center.

Chapter 8

Grigsby, William, and Stephen J. Goetz. 2004. "Telehealth: What Promises
Does It Hold for Rural Areas?" In *Critical Issues in Rural Health*, edited
by Nina Glasgow, Lois Wright Morton, and Nan E. Johnson, 237–50.
Ames, Iowa: Blackwell Publishing.

Hu, Elise. 2016. "Golden Years, Iron Bars: Japan Sees Rise In Crime By The
Elderly." NPR. Accessed May 25, 2021. https://www.npr.org/sections/
parallels/2016/11/22/500040363/golden-years-iron-bars-japan-sees-rise-
in-crime-by-the-elderly.

Kawachi, Ichiro, Bruce P. Kennedy, and Roberta Glass. 1999. "Social
Capital and Self-Rated Health: A Contextual Analysis." *American*
Journal of Public Health 89 (8): 1187–93. https://doi.org/10.2105/
AJPH.89.8.1187.

Kawanehonchō Office. 2017. "Staitstics of Kawanehonchō." Accessed May
25, 2021. http://www.town.kawanehon.shizuoka.jp/material/files/
group/1/2017-5nennreibetsujinkou.pdf.

Chapter 9

AARP. 2019. "How Continuing Care Retirement Communities Work." Accessed May 25, 2021. https://www.aarp.org/caregiving/basics/ info-2017/continuing-care-retirement-communities.html.

Abe, Ryosuke. 2015. "*Kōreisha ijū kousou* (Plan for CCRC in Japan)." Mainichi Shimbun, December 8, 2015.

Brown, David L. and Nina Glasgow. 2008. *Rural Retirement Migration*. New York: Springer.

Cross Media Shimada. 2018. "Coconage Magazine." *NPR Cross Media Shimada*, June, 2018.

Flora, Corneria Butler, Jan L. Flora, and Stephen P. Gasteyer. 2018. *Rural Communities*. 4th ed. Routledge.

Groger, Lisa and Jennifer Kinney. 2007. "CCRC Here We Come! Reasons for Moving to a Continuing Care Retirement Community." *Journal of Housing For the Elderly*. 4: 79–101. https://doi.org/10.1300/J081v20n04_ 06.

Ijyuu-life kenkyū-kai. 2016. *Kazokude chiho ijyuu hajimemashita: Ikikata wo kaetai imadoki kosodate sedai no sentaku (Young Families Moving to Rural Areas)*. Tokyo, Japan: Yousensha.

Isa, Tomomi. 2017. *Ijyuu joshi (Japanese Women Migrating to Rural Areas)*. Tokyo, Japan: Shinchousha.

Kawanehonchō Office. 2018. *Datsu nichijou Kawanehonchō* (Town to Get Away from Your Busy Life). Kawanehonchō: Kawanehonchō Municipal Government.

Kawanehonchō Office. 2021. "Staitstics of Kawanehonchō." Accessed May 25, 2021. Retrieved May 25, 2021. http://www.town.kawanehon.shizuoka.jp/chosei/14/index.html.

Kimura, Kyoko. 2015. *Senior no chihou ijyu sanpi wakareru* (Debates over the Senior Migration). *Nihon Keizai Shimbun*, June 25, 2015.

Masuda, Hiroya. 2015. *Tokyo shōmetsu (Limit of Tokyo in Supporting the Elderly and Rural Migration)*. Tokyo, Japan: Chūkō Shinsho.

Matsuda, Tomoo. 2017. *Nihonban CCRC ga wakaru hon (Overview of CCRC in Japan)*. Tokyo: Houken.

Matsuda, Tsutomu. 1998. *Shūmatsu wa inaka gurashi (Living in Rural Home for the Weekend)*. Tokyo, Japan: Soushinsha.

OZmall. 2015. "Jimoto Trip Vol. 1 (Local Trip Vol.1)." *OZmall*. Retrieved October 11, 2018 http://www.ozmall.co.jp/travel/feature/2881/.

Shizuoka Prefecture Homepage. 2012. "Yutorisuto No. 93." *Yutorisuto Shizuoka*. Retrieved October 11, 2018. https://iju.pref.shizuoka.jp/.

Sugihara, Shiho and Gary W. Evans. 2000. "Place Attachment and Social Support at Continuing Care Retirement Communities." *Environment and Behavior* 32 (3): 400–9. https://doi.org/10.1177/00139160021972 586.

Tamamura, Tomio. 2007. *Inakagurashi ga dekiru hito dekinai hito (People Who Can Migrate to Rural Areas and Those Who Cannot)*. Tokyo, Japan: Shueisha.

Tawara, Moeko. 2000. *Watashi no inaka gurashi (My Rural Lifestyle)*. Tokyo, Japan: Daiwa Shobo.

Tomoeda, Kojiro. 2016. *Shūmatsu ijyūkara hajimeyou (Let's Start Living in Rural Areas for Weekend)*. Tokyo, Japan: Soshisha.

Tsuchiya, Sakka. 2018. "Women's Choice." *Shizuoka Shimbun*, June 4.

Yamada, Taku. 2018. *Gaikokujin ga nekkyou suru cool na inaka no tsukuri-kata (Ways to Renovate Rural Towns to Attract Foreigners)*. Tokyo, Japan: Shinchōsha.

Yamamoto, Kazunori. 1999. *Sanzan hataraitekita kara teinengo wa fuufu de inakagurashi (Rural Retirement Migration)*. Tokyo, Japan: Yosensha.

Yamazaki, Takeya. 2009. *Senior koso tokai ni sumou (It's Better for the Elderly to Live in Urban Areas)*. Tokyo, Japan: PHP Interface.

Chapter 10

Brooke, Joanne, and Debra Jackson. 2020. "Older People and COVID-19: Isolation, Risk and Ageism." *Journal of Clinical Nursing* 29 (13–14): 2044–46. https://doi.org/10.1111/jocn.15274.

Brown, David L., and Nina Glasgow. 2008. *Rural Retirement Migration*. New York: Springer.

Burnes, David, Christine Sheppard, Charles R. Henderson, Monica Wassel, Richenda Cope, Chantal Barber, and Karl Pillemer. 2019. "Interventions to Reduce Ageism against Older Adults: A Systematic Review and Meta-Analysis." *American Journal of Public Health* 109 (8): e1-e9. https://doi.org/10.2105/AJPH.2019.305123.

Hagestad, Gunhild O., and Peter Uhlenberg. 2005. "The Social Separation of Old and Young: A Root of Ageism." *Journal of Social Issues* 61(2): 343–60. https://doi.org/10.1111/j.1540-4560.2005.00409.x.

The Japan Times. 2020. "70% in Japan Want Telecommuning to Continue after Pandemic, Survey Finds." Accessed May 25, 2020. https://www.japantimes.co.jp/news/2020/06/22/business/japan-telecommuting-continue/.

Kawanehonchō Office. 2018. "Kawanehonchō Guidebook for Newcomers (in Japanese)." Accessed May 25, 2020. http://www.town.kawanehon.shizuoka.jp/soshiki/kikaku/kikakutyosei/6267.html.

Klinenberg, Eric. 2003. *Heat Wave: A Social Autopsy of Disaster in Chicago.* University of Chicago Press.

Knight, John. 2003. "Repopulating the Village?" In *Demographic Change and the Family in Japan's Aging Society*, edited by John W. Traphagan and John Knight, 107–23. New York: State University of New York Press.

Kumagai, Fumie. 2014. "International Marriage in Japan: A Strategy to Maintain Rural Farm Households." In *Family Issues on Marriage, Divorce, and Older Adults In Japan*, 65–88. Singapore: Springer.

Kyocera Communication Systems. 2016. "The Use of High-Speed Internet in Town (in Japanese)." Accessed May 25, 2021. https://www.kccs.co.jp/com-engineering/case/0003/.

Losada-Baltar, Andrés, Lucía Jiménez-Gonzalo, Laura Gallego-Alberto, María Del Sequeros Pedroso-Chaparro, José Fernandes-Pires, and María Márquez-González. 2020. "'We're Staying at Home'. Association of Self-Perceptions of Aging, Personal and Family Resources and Loneliness with Psychological Distress during the Lock-down Period of COVID-19." *The Journals of Gerontology. Series B, Psychological Sciences and Social Sciences* 76 (2): e10-e16. https://doi.org/10.1093/geronb/gbaa048.

Manton, Kenneth G., and James W. Vaupel. 1995. "Survival after the Age of 80 in the United States, Sweden, France, England, and Japan." *New England Journal of Medicine* 333: 1232–35. https://doi.org/10.1056/NEJM199511023331824.

Matsumoto, Masatoshi, Keisuke Takeuchi, Junko Tanaka, Susumu Tazuma, Kazuo Inoue, Tetsuhiro Owaki, Seitaro Iguchi, and Takahiro Maeda. 2016. "Follow-up Study of the Regional Quota System of Japanese Medical Schools and Prefecture Scholarship Programmes: A Study Protocol." *BMJ Open* 6: e011165. https://doi.org/10.1136/bmjopen-2016-011165.

The Shizuoka Shimbun. 2021a. "The first case of Covid-19 in Kawanehonchō." March 31, 2021.

———. 2021b. "COVID-19 cases in Shizuoka Prefecture". Retrieved June 15, 2021. https://www.at-s.com/news/article/health/shizuoka/752659.html.

Skoufalos, Alexis, Janice L. Clarke, Dana Rose Ellis, Vicki L. Shepard, and Elizabeth Y. Rula. 2017. "Rural Aging in America: Proceedings of the 2017 Connectivity Summit." *Population Health Management* 20 (Supplement 2): S1–S10. https://doi.org/10.1089/pop.2017.0177.

Sugimoto, Yoshio. 2014. *An Introduction to Japanese Society.* Cambridge University Press.

Yamamoto, Kana, Akihiko Ozaki, Morihito Takita, Tomohiro Morita, Hiroyuki Saito, Yuki Senoo, Tetsuya Tanimoto, and Masahiro Kami. 2019. "Negative Aspects of the Regional Quota System in Japan." *Japan Medical Association Journal* 2 (1): 85–86. https://www.jmaj.jp/detail.php?id=10.31662%2Fjmaj.2018-0055.

Index

activities of daily living (ADLs), 14,
51, 92, 102, 104
aging in place (age in place), 13, 15,
17, 18, 55, 56, 73, 85, 109
Aurora, Nebraska 42, 128

below the replacement level (below-
replacement fertility rate), 6, 8,
128
Bourdieu, Pierre, 42
bride drought, 8
bride famine, 8

cancer, 58, 64, 73
calligraphy, 33, 35, 77, 78, 98
care manager, 49, 57, 68, 69, 71–73,
76, 87, 89, 90, 92–94
Carer's café (caretaker's café), 32,
49, 67, 75, 76, 92
census-survival rate (forward)
method, 28
Chicago Heat Wave, 131
China, 137
circular migrants, 122
collective efficacy, 36, 38–40, 44, 45,
51, 57, 65, 66, 81, 85, 95, 104,
106, 110, 111, 129, 130–132, 136

collectivism, 108
community-based integrated care
system, 15, 16
Continuing Care Retirement
Communities (CCRCs),
117–119, 128
Cornell Retirement Migration
Survey, 42
COVID-19, 130, 132, 134, 135
crime, 32, 38–40, 106, 131
crisis of care, 22
Cyprus, 118

depopulation, 4, 10–13, 16–19, 22,
23, 89, 93, 107, 109–111, 125,
128–132, 134, 136, 137
dialect, 69, 70, 71, 79, 83, 92, 124,
136
Durkheim, Émile, 37, 38, 42

eldest son, 3, 4, 21, 103, 105, 120
England, 43, 44, 129
entrepreneurial social infrastructure (ESI), 42
Europe, 118, 126, 129

festivals, 78–80, 83, 88, 89, 95, 99,
    101, 106, 133
filial piety, 10
funeral, 116
France, 6–8, 125, 129

Gardening (garden), 32, 35, 59, 65,
    68, 74, 78, 91, 106, 109, 123, 127,
    136
GDP, 15
Gemeinschaft, 42
Gender Inequality Index (GII), 7
Generalized reciprocity, 74, 83, 85,
genkai shūraku, 12, 13, 18
Genki Hatsuratsu Kyōshitsu, 48, 49,
    67, 72
Genki-up, 49, 67, 83
Germany, 8
Gesellschaft, 42
grassroots, 17, 56, 84,
Great Heisei Era Amalgamation
    Initiative, 12
green tea, 22, 25, 26, 60, 64, 75, 80,
    82, 84, 88–91, 94, 95, 127, 130,
    132
Gross national product, 4
ground golf, 35, 124

hard development, 11, 12
healthy aging, 13, 19, 28, 30, 33, 48,
    49, 53, 66, 67, 85, 104, 111, 133,
healthy life expectancy (Otasshado),
    28, 111, 130
hot spring, 26, 32, 75, 84, 118, 120,
    121

I-turn, 112, 117
I-turner, 112, 119, 121, 124, 127
ibasho (the place we belong), 35, 50

ie system, 3, 4, 21, 105
ikigai (the purpose of life), 51, 76,
    81, 84, 108, 109
Ikigai Day Service, 48, 49, 67, 76, 77,
    90
inaka, 112
industrialization, 4, 5
informal social control, 39, 40, 65,
    106, 107, 111
infrastructure, 11, 12, 42, 128
Instrumental Activities of Daily
    Living (IADLs), 102, 104
Italy, 8, 118

Kamikatsuchō, 17
Kawanehonchō, 12, 19, 22–35, 45,
    47–49, 51–53, 57, 63–68, 70–74,
    76, 78, 82–85, 87, 89–95, 98,
    103, 104, 106, 109–112
Kawanehonchō Council of Social
    Welfare (KCSW), 31, 33–35,
    47–49, 51–57, 64, 67, 74, 76, 78,
    79, 81, 84, 87–89, 92, 93, 95, 97,
    99, 105, 106, 111, 119, 124
Kawanehonchō municipal welfare
    office, 31, 32, 47, 48, 52, 67, 95,
    97, 111, 119, 124
Kawane-phone, 130, 131
Kawauchi Village, 17

life course, 89, 91, 108, 110, 123
lifestyle, 33, 43, 48, 84, 90, 110, 112,
    114, 123, 134
living alone, 5, 10, 18, 50, 54, 75, 93,
    98, 104–106, 124, 131
lonely, 93, 100, 107
Long term care insurance (LTCI),
    13–16, 30, 31, 73, 104
longitudinal, 44, 128, 137

Maine, 129, 133
Malaysia, 22
mechanical solidarity, 38, 42
medical school, 134
Meiji Civil Code, 3
Meiji Restoration, 3
membership, 42, 43, 81, 83, 84, 124
merger, 18, 95, 111
minsei-iin, 79, 87
multigenerational, 118
Municipal employees, 32, 51, 68–76, 84, 87, 91, 92, 97, 105, 106, 130

Nanmokumura, 18
Naturally Occuring Retirement Community (NORC), 119, 128
Neighborhood association, 99, 107, 116,
non-profit organization, 32, 35, 51, 92, 119, 123
norms of reciprocity, 41, 88
North Korea, 137

omotenashi, 88
organic solidarity, 38
Organization for Economic Cooperation and Development (OECD), 6, 15
origami, 33, 77, 98, 116
otagaisama, 74, 83, 85, 87–89, 95, 111
outsider, 42, 83, 84, 88, 92, 116, 123, 128, 133

permaculture, 112, 127
Philippines, 7, 137
positive thinking, 65
primogeniture, 3, 4, 105
pull factor, 4, 136

push factor, 3

qualitative, 44, 45, 47, 49, 52, 136, 137
quality of life, 72, 73, 130
quoits tournament, 49, 67, 81, 82

requiring care levels, 14, 30, 55, 87
requiring support levels, 14, 16, 30, 55, 87, 104
retirement migration (retirement migrants), 42, 51, 118, 119, 128
returnee, 119
ryōsai kenbo, 4

salon, 33–35, 48, 53, 67, 68, 74–76, 79–81, 87–89, 91, 92, 94, 95
seasonal, 79, 80, 88, 133
Second World War, 4, 5, 19, 21, 22, 25
seken, 10, 70, 119
self-rated health, 43, 44, 51, 62, 65, 102
shakyō, 31
shrine, 89, 116
social capital, 10, 17, 36, 38–45, 51, 57, 66, 104, 110, 136
bonding social capital, 42, 64, 73, 104, 130–132, 135
bridging social capital, 42, 64, 104, 128, 135, 136
cognitive social capital, 41, 43, 74, 110, 111
horizontal social capital, 41, 56
structural social capital, 41, 43, 44, 68, 110
vertical social capital, 41
social cohesion, 37–40, 65, 106, 107, 110, 111

social infertility, 6
social integration, 10, 16, 37, 111, 133
social isolation, 55, 69, 84, 85, 87, 105, 106
social network, 10, 41, 42, 81, 84, 87, 110
socioeconomic status (SES), 37, 39, 43, 66, 106, 129, 131, 136
soft development, 11, 12
South Korea, 7, 12, 137
Spain, 22, 118
subculture, 119
sumiyoi, 109, 110
Sweden, 7, 8, 15, 129

Takasuchō, 17
telecommuting, 134
telemedicine, 109
three-generation, 10, 57, 63, 137
Tönnies, Ferdinand, 42
Total Fertility Rate (TFR), 5–7

traditional, 3–5, 10, 22, 124, 133, 134, 137
trust, 38–41, 43, 60, 64, 65, 73, 87, 97, 110, 136

ubasute, 118
urbanization, 4, 5, 16, 64, 117
U.K., 12
U.S., 4, 6–8, 12, 15, 22, 78, 118, 129

vegetables, 18, 59, 65, 74, 78, 82, 83, 91, 105–107, 109, 112, 113, 116, 123, 125, 127
vitality, 12, 84, 111
volunteer, 43, 54, 57, 61, 68, 83, 88, 99, 118

Western (West), 3, 5, 7, 8, 37, 45, 65

yakuba, 31
Yazuchō, 18
Yume no Tsuribashi, 26